P9-DOF-562

Fifth Edition

Handle with Care

Communicating in the Human Services Field in Canada

Lucy Valentino
Humber College Institute of Technology
and Advanced Learning

WITHDRAWN SEP 17 2014

PROPERTY OF
SENECA COLLEGE
LIBRARIES
YORKGATE CAMPUS

NELSON / **E D U C A T I O N**

NELSON / EDUCATION

Handle with Care: Communicating in the Human
Services Field in Canada, Fifth Edition
by Lucy Valentino

**Vice President, Editorial
Higher Education:**
Anne Williams

Acquisitions Editor:
Anne-Marie Taylor

Marketing Manager:
Ann Byford

Developmental Editor:
Liisa Kelly

Permissions Coordinator:
Daniela Glass

Production Service:
Cenveo Publisher Services

Copy Editor:
Erin Moore

Proofreader:
Elizabeth Phinney

Indexer:
Robert Swanson

Senior Production Coordinator:
Ferial Suleman

Design Director:
Ken Phipps

Managing Designer:
Franca Amore

Interior Design:
Peggy Rhodes

Chapter Opener Image:
Sveta Demidoff/Getty Images

Cover Design:
Jennifer Stimson

Cover Image:
David Jordan Williams/Getty
Images

Compositor:
Cenveo Publisher Services

Printer:
RR Donnelley

COPYRIGHT © 2013, 2009 by
Nelson Education Ltd.

Printed and bound in the
United States
4 15 14

For more information contact
Nelson Education Ltd.,
1120 Birchmount Road, Toronto,
Ontario, M1K 5G4. Or you can
visit our Internet site at
http://www.nelson.com

Statistics Canada information
is used with the permission
of Statistics Canada. Users are
forbidden to copy this material
and/or redisseminate the data, in
an original or modified form, for
commercial purposes, without the
expressed permissions of Statistics
Canada. Information on the
availability of the wide range of
data from Statistics Canada can be
obtained from Statistics Canada's
Regional Offices, its World Wide
Web site at <http://www.statcan.
gc.ca>, and its toll-free access
number 1-800-263-1136.

ALL RIGHTS RESERVED. No part
of this work covered by the copyright herein may be reproduced,
transcribed, or used in any form
or by any means—graphic, electronic, or mechanical, including
photocopying, recording, taping,
Web distribution, or information
storage and retrieval systems—
without the written permission
of the publisher.

For permission to use material
from this text or product,
submit all requests online at
www.cengage.com/permissions.
Further questions about
permissions can be emailed to
permissionrequest@cengage.com

Every effort has been made to
trace ownership of all copyrighted
material and to secure permission
from copyright holders. In the
event of any question arising as
to the use of any material, we will
be pleased to make the necessary
corrections in future printings.

**Library and Archives Canada
Cataloguing in Publication**

Valentino, Lucy, 1952-

Handle with care: communicating
in the human services field in
Canada/Lucy Valentino.—5th ed.

Includes index.
ISBN 978-0-17-650439-7

1. Social case work reporting—
Textbooks. 2. Proposal writing
in human services—Textbooks.
3. Communication in human
services—Textbooks. 4. English
language—Composition and
exercises—Textbooks. I. Title.

HV43.V35 2012 808.06'6361
C2011-907348-X

ISBN-10: 0-17-650439-7
ISBN-13: 978-0-17-650439-7

CONTENTS

HOW TO USE THIS TEXT

This text has grown out of my experiences teaching report writing to students in several human services programs at two Toronto colleges. It can be used for both individual and collaborative writing. The discussion in the text is built upon an inductive approach: rather than providing students with a structure for a specific type of writing, a structure they are then expected to follow blindly, I begin with a writing situation and discuss the process of discovering the structure needed based on the writer's purpose and audience, as well as the context of the communication act. I do provide a summary of some standard structures, but the ultimate object of this text is not to provide cookie-cutter blueprints but to enable students to discover an appropriate structure in any writing situation.

The text is built upon the practice of collaborative writing, although a teacher who favours a noncollaborative approach can still use the Explorations as individual writing assignments. (Actually, as discussed in the Instructor's Manual, the most fruitful approach is probably a combination of collaborative and individual writing.) Collaborative writing is done by pairs or small groups of students. Students are given a writing assignment (either the term-long project or a one-hour Exploration). They discuss the assignment and do the writing collaboratively.

The collaborative approach is useful for many reasons. When students graduate, they will often find themselves in situations in the field where they are expected to work collaboratively; even if the final writing is sometimes done individually, a human services worker relies on colleagues for feedback, advice, the voice of experience, and so on. Except in a traditional school setting, people do not work in a vacuum. It is sometimes difficult for students to make the transition to a world where asking another person for help is not considered cheating, where colleagues function as members of a team.

Collaborative writing provides a chance to learn and exercise a valuable skill.

Collaborative writing also offers the opportunity for students to synthesize their knowledge of the field they have been studying. The Explorations not only exercise the students' writing skills but also offer them an opportunity to think about the situations given and to discuss issues of practice in their field. Working collaboratively, students can debate (often quite heatedly) what the correct approach might be in the given situation. They sometimes find that there are several possible approaches rather than one right answer. The Explorations are deliberately somewhat sketchy. I expect my students to "invent" some of the missing details, based on their experience (or, if necessary, library or Internet research). This encourages ownership of the writing process. The final form the Exploration takes is itself a collaborative effort.

The most significant reason for a collaborative approach has to do with the student–teacher relationship. Students know who holds the power of the mark; no matter how open or democratic a classroom, the students know the underlying power structure. When a teacher offers a suggestion for revision, a student will often accept that suggestion *uncritically* (not always, but often). The revision is made in the work without learning taking place. On the other hand, when a collaborative writing partner disagrees with a strategy or rejects a wording, dialogue follows. I have been amazed at the discussions that have taken place in a collaborative writing group and the learning that has ensued.

There are some pitfalls to collaborative writing. The writings should be done in class, for the most part, so that the groups can be monitored by the teacher. Groups must learn to stay on task, and the teacher should try to ensure that all members are contributing. To ensure that the stronger writers are not carrying the weaker ones, some Explorations should be done individually. The members of a group may have a disagreement that they can't resolve about a particular Exploration. I encourage the members to agree to disagree, and I expect two reports, one by the majority and another by the dissenters.

One last note: The Explorations cover many areas of human services. I have found that students enjoy doing Explorations outside their area of specialization as well. I would urge you to give them the opportunity to transfer their skills to a situation from another area. This is also good preparation for the real world, where people's needs are not so neatly compartmentalized.

The Instructor's Manual offers further suggestions. I hope you enjoy this approach.

This updated edition includes updated coverage of the Personal Information Protection and Electronic Documents Act (PIPEDA), expanded coverage of memos, e-mails, and letters, a discussion of social networking, and many new explorations for writing. The publishers and I hope that you will enjoy this new edition of *Handle with Care*.

A NOTE TO THE STUDENT

This text does not have all the answers.

What do I mean by that statement? After all, considering what you paid for this text, you deserve all the answers, don't you?

Not if you want to learn to communicate well.

This text is a guidebook. We'll walk together through several communication situations. I'll share some of my experiences with you, and then you will be left to explore for yourself. You won't be alone, because this text is built on the principle of collaboration—your fellow students will help you find your way.

I cannot teach you to communicate well, but you can learn to do so. I can only offer advice and give you opportunities to practise. So, while you will find some suggestions in this text, do not follow them slavishly. With your fellow students, discuss the situations, using your knowledge and experience to adapt or modify the advice to your needs.

You have the answers. Find them together.

ACKNOWLEDGMENTS

I thank my colleagues at Humber College, especially Eva Bednar and Sarah Armenia, who provided feedback as they taught using the text and who gave me permission to include some of their ideas for Explorations. I am grateful to the editorial staff at Nelson for their support. It has been a pleasure to work with such a professional, knowledgable, and gracious group of people. Thanks especially to Anne-Marie Taylor (Acquisitions Editor), Liisa Kelly (Developmental Editor), Susan Calvert (Director, Content and Media Production), Erin Moore (Copy Editor), Elizabeth Phinney (Proofreader), Ferial Suleman (Senior Production Coordinator), Ann Byford (Marketing Manager), and Daniela Glass (Permissions Coordinator). And thank-you to past and current students, who have taught me so much.

This edition is dedicated to Avery Kenneth and Keira Teresa Wills. May you learn, grow, and carry joy with you always.

CHAPTER 1

PURPOSE AND AUDIENCE

Overview: This chapter discusses purpose and audience. Writers need to be aware of why they are writing (purpose) and who is going to be reading what they have written (audience). One way to develop a sense of both purpose and audience is to practise by presenting essentially the same material to different audiences. The new purpose and new audience call for different communication strategies.

PURPOSE

Why do we write anything? Take a few minutes to list all the writing you have done in the past three days. Your list might look something like this:

- homework for PSYC 106
- note to John to buy milk
- notes in English class
- e-mail to Gita
- words to a song I've been working on
- list of what I had to do yesterday
- rough draft of research essay for RL245
- several pages in my journal
- memo to supervisor at work asking for time off during exam week
- text message to Chris during last class: skip this one?

What do the items on your list have in common? They certainly differ in many ways. My hypothetical list, for example, contains items that would have been dashed off (text message, note to buy milk), items that took some thought but were still informal (list of what I had to do, e-mail to a friend, class notes, journal, homework), and items that would take more time and effort (memo to supervisor, words to song, rough draft of essay). What each piece of writing has in common is that it was written for a purpose and for an audience. How I approached each writing task was dictated (for the most part unconsciously) by what I wanted to achieve and for whom I was writing.

AUDIENCE

The informal, dashed-off messages held an instrumental purpose: I simply wanted to get something done, in a quick, economical way. Yet how I wrote the messages depended on my relationship with the person getting the note, what I knew about that person, and so on. Consider, for example, the different ways I might write a note asking John to pick up milk, depending on my relationship with him:

"Dear John—Get milk."
"John-John—Out of milk again. Can you pick
some up? Love ya."
"John—You finished all the milk again. PLEASE
pick some up before I get home."

Even writing that you do for yourself has both purpose and audience. You are the audience. Your purpose can be instrumental (remembering what you have to do, getting down the main points of a lecture) or more reflective (journal writing, creative writing).

Every piece of written communication has both purpose and audience. Problems arise when we forget, or never bother to determine, why we are writing and whom we want to reach with that writing. Most of us have times when we suffer from logorrhea, or diarrhea of the mouth, when we get so full of ourselves that we forget to communicate. We forget that we are writing for a purpose, a purpose that can be achieved only by communicating with our audience.

It is crucial that we be aware of our purpose and audience. Let me give you an example from my experience with early childhood education (ECE) students. The students had prepared a daycare policies and procedures manual in another course. For my class, I asked them to use that manual for raw material in writing a parent handbook.

A few students simply took the manual, changed the cover page, and handed it in as a parent handbook. A few others dropped the sections relating to terminating a worker, and so on, but kept such sections as "What to do in cases of staff sexual abuse of children" and "What to do if a child dies at the daycare centre."

The first group made a basic mistake in failing to consider me as an audience. With any assignment, a student might be assumed to have at least two purposes: to learn something and to get a good mark. Neither purpose was likely to be achieved by their approach. They didn't do the assignment, so they couldn't learn anything. Probably more important, from the students' perspective, they couldn't achieve a good mark, because I had seen the manuals and therefore knew they had done no work on this assignment.

Although the second group got a bit closer to the spirit of the assignment, they too made an elementary mistake with respect to their audience. The supposed audience for a parent handbook is the parents of the children in a centre. If you were a parent, how would you react to seeing a section on possible sexual abuse by a staff member? Speaking for myself, I would find another centre.

A third group of students was able to make the transition to an audience-centred handbook. They thought about their material from the parents' point of view and then presented everything the parents needed, but nothing more. Rather than directing their writing to other ECE professionals, they wrote for their audience—the parents of the children in the centre. They communicated with their audience.

Of course, students are not the only ones who have difficulty with this skill. Many people are blind to audience or have a warped sense of who their audience is. For example, consider how some adults speak to children. There is a certain tone of voice that some adults use, an octave higher and cute as a button, as though they were talking to little runaways from Oz. I have a friend my children adored because she spoke to them as though she were speaking to adults—in a normal pitch, and as though she expected to hear a rational reply. Having a clear sense of audience often means simply respecting those with whom you are communicating—by accepting them as equals and talking to them without being condescending.

AN EXERCISE IN ESTABLISHING PURPOSE AND AUDIENCE

Having a sense of purpose and audience is a skill that can be developed and practised. Let's work through an example. Here is your raw material:

You are the supervisor of a group home for developmentally delayed adolescents. The purpose of the home is to prepare these young adults for community living, either in a group home or on their own, at some time in the future.

Jerry F., age 16, is one of the adolescents living in the group home. He comes from a musical family and has been a member of a local church choir for the year he has been with you. He has enjoyed the experience, but for the past few months there has been a problem. There are several girls that are Jerry's age in the choir, and Jerry has been behaving inappropriately by touching them, stroking their hair, and so on. He appears to be attracted to one girl in particular, Lisa R.

Although you have held counselling sessions with Jerry, he has continued to act inappropriately, despite the girls' complaints and warnings from the choir's director. On March 3 the director, Étienne F., warned you that if the behaviour continued, Jerry would not be allowed to continue with the choir. You discussed this warning with Jerry, and he was very anxious to remain a choir member. However, on March 10 he kissed Lisa R. against her will. Mr. F. immediately escorted Jerry back to the group home and explained to him that his behaviour was unacceptable and that he could not come back to the choir.

Let's use this material to write two different documents: (1) an incident report for Jerry's file and (2) a letter to Jerry's parents explaining why he may no longer continue in the choir.

How would these communications be different?

First, consider the incident report. What is the purpose? This report would probably have two purposes:

- to document the incident
- to provide a basis for a treatment goal for Jerry

Who is the audience? You and other professionals dealing with Jerry.

What type of language is appropriate? The professional language of the field, expressed clearly, precisely, and succinctly.

What exactly would your audience, your reader, want to know?

- who Jerry is
- what led up to the incident (including prior behaviour and counselling)
- what happened exactly
- what is being done as follow-up

Now consider the letter to Jerry's parents. What is the purpose?

- to let them know why Jerry cannot continue in the choir
- to assure them that their son will be all right

Who is the audience? Jerry's parents, who love and care about their son. They are anxious and concerned, and they need your reassurance.

What type of language is appropriate? Clear, simple, non-patronizing language, free of jargon.

What exactly would Jerry's parents want to know?

- how their son is doing overall
- what happened
- what you are doing to help their son

The resulting communications might look like those on pages 7 to 9.

INCIDENT REPORT

Name: Jerry F.
Age: 16
Residence: Westfield Group Home
Date of Admission: March 1, 2010

Jerry F. is a 16-year-old resident of Westfield Group Home. He has resided at the home since March 1, 2010, in preparation for community living.

Jerry enjoys music very much and has been a member of the St. Cecilia Church Choir since March 5, 2010. He has adjusted well to choir routines, but in December 2010 choir director Étienne F. reported problems with Jerry's inappropriate behaviour. Jerry is experiencing normal adolescent sexual feelings, but he is having difficulty dealing with these feelings in an age-appropriate manner. Specifically, he has on several occasions touched adolescent female members of the choir, albeit in a nonsexual way, stroking their hair, touching their arms, etc. In response to their and Mr. F's complaints, I counselled Jerry re: his sexual feelings and their appropriate expression. He continued to have difficulty modifying his behaviour, and Mr. F. contacted me on March 3, stating that if such behaviour continued, Jerry would be barred from the choir.

On March 10, Jerry kissed a female choir member, Lisa R., and was escorted back to the home by Mr. F., who told him he could not return to the choir. Jerry appeared ambivalent; my impression was that he felt both empowered by and guilty for what he had done. I explored the incident with Jerry, but he does not seem to grasp that he will not be allowed to return to the choir.

Further sexuality counselling is required. Jerry's activities should be designed to include age-appropriate recreation with adolescent girls in a controlled environment. He also needs to be reminded of the difference between culturally appropriate and inappropriate touching.

Date: March 11, 2011
Time: 9:05 a.m.
Signed:

Mario Ricci

Mario Ricci, DSW

LETTER TO PARENTS

Westfield Group Home
2345 Lakeview Road
Sudbury, Ontario
P3A 3F8

March 11, 2011

Sam and Mary Feinster
1427 Shore Breeze Drive
Sudbury, Ontario
P3A 1D6

Dear Mr. and Mrs. Feinster:

Your son, Jerry, has been adjusting well to life in Westfield Group Home. He has taken on several responsibilities, such as caring for his room and possessions, sharing the chores of setting and clearing the table, and taking his turn once a week in helping to make dinner. However, he is having difficulty in one area, though one that is not uncommon for boys his age, whatever their circumstances.

As you know, Jerry has been a member of the St. Cecilia Church Choir for the past year. He has enjoyed practising and singing each week and, until recently, has fit in well with the rest of the choir. However, Jerry is having difficulty relating with the girls of his own age in the choir. We have been discussing what is and is not acceptable behaviour, but the girls have repeatedly complained over the past three months that Jerry is bothering them, touching their arms, stroking their hair, and so on. The choir director let me know how Jerry was behaving, and I talked with Jerry about his behaviour several times. It is difficult for him to understand that, although he merely wants to make contact with these girls by touching them, the girls do not want him to do so.

On March 10, Jerry kissed one of the girls in choir and was told by the director that he could no longer be a member, since he had already been warned several times about his behaviour. Though Jerry will miss being in the choir, we are planning alternative activities for him. We will be working on having him take part in activities with girls of his own age so that he can become comfortable with his feelings and express them in acceptable ways.

Jerry's present difficulties are a normal part of adolescence. We will provide him with the help he needs to get through this phase. If you have any questions or concerns, please do not hesitate to call me at 243-6534.

Sincerely,

Mario Ricci

Mario Ricci, DSW

(I assume that Jerry gave Mario permission to share this information with Jerry's parents.)

SUMMARY

Incident Report

Purpose: to document incident
Audience: other professionals
Structure:

    I.   Identification of characteristics of client involved
    II.   Background to incident
    III. Description of incident
    IV. Follow-up to incident

Letter to Parents

Purpose: to inform Jerry's parents of incident without unduly alarming them
Audience: Jerry's parents
Structure:

    I.   Opening stressing overall progress
    II.   Background to incident
    III. Incident itself
    IV. Reassurance

Now it's your turn to practise. You may do the following exercises in groups, as collaborative writing, or alone. With each exercise, keep in mind why you are writing and who your reader is.

(Note: A more complete discussion of letter format takes place in Chapter 3.)

EXPLORATIONS

1.1 You work in a group home for adolescent young offenders. On January 5, two residents, David R. and Amin P., were involved in a fistfight in the TV room over which show to watch. Along with counsellor Larry Stoltzman, you were able to break up the fight, but not before two lamps were broken and David R. received a black eye. Follow-up interviews with the boys revealed prior friction over Amanda S., a girl at school. Amin P. has a history of fighting, both at school and in the group home.

> a. Write an incident report to be placed in the home's files.
> b. Switch perspectives. You are the director of the home. Write a letter to the father of Amin P. (his mother is deceased), alerting him to his son's continued aggression.

1.2 You are the director of a day treatment centre for patients with Alzheimer's disease. Mrs. Molly T., who is in the second stage of Alzheimer's, has been with your centre for the past six months. You have just reviewed her progress with your staff. *(Note: If you are unfamiliar with Alzheimer's disease, you will need to do library or Internet research to complete this Exploration.)*

> a. Write a progress report to be placed in Molly T.'s file. (See Chapter 4 for the structure of a progress report.)
> b. Write a letter to Molly T.'s family, summarizing her progress.

1.3 You are the manager of Crescent Road Community Centre, a publicly funded complex, which includes swimming facilities, meeting rooms, an indoor shuffleboard court, and an ice-skating rink. During public skating time, a nine-year-old skater, Sumitra S., was jostled by a group of four adolescent boys who were playing tag on the ice, despite a posted rule forbidding game playing. She was knocked over and broke her fall with her hand. Sumitra's parents were present and took her to Westford Hospital to have the hand and forearm X-rayed. The X-rays revealed that she had fractured her wrist. Doctors wrapped the wrist in an elastic bandage and had her return the following morning to have the bone reset under general anaesthetic.

> a. Write an incident report for the centre's files.
> b. Signs posted in the ice rink warn that violation of the rules will result in loss of use privileges. Write a letter to the four boys, temporarily suspending them from using the ice rink.
> c. Write a letter to Sumitra and her parents regarding the incident.

1.4 You are the supervisor of a daycare centre that has just undergone its yearly governmental inspection. The inspector told you that the centre has inadequate outdoor play equipment. Unless this situation is corrected, the licensing body will revoke the centre's licence. The centre does not have the money at present to buy more equipment.

    a. Write a letter to the licensing body to buy more time while you raise the money.

    b. Write a letter to parents with children in the centre, explaining the situation and requesting their help in fund-raising.

1.5 You are a DSW working with a developmentally delayed child who is mainstreamed in a grade 3 classroom. Your major goal with the child, Amy C., has been to teach her to read. She has made great progress and can now read the first reader in the grade 1 series.

    a. Summarize Amy's progress for her Individualized Planning file.

    b. Write a letter to Amy's parents bringing them up to date on her progress.

1.6 You are the supervisor of a group home for adolescent girls who have been involved with drugs. House rules prohibit both alcohol and drug use. Mandy L., age 15, was missing at lights-out on August 14; when she appeared at 5:00 a.m., August 15, she was drunk and in possession of a small quantity of cocaine. She refused to answer any questions and was aggressive. The next morning she was uncooperative. This is the second time Mandy has violated this house rule.

    a. Write an incident report for Mandy's file.

    b. Write a letter to Mandy's parents, explaining that she may no longer stay in your group home because of her noncompliance and that she is being transferred to another setting.

1.7 You are the executive director of a group of franchised daycare centres. One area of town has had an outbreak of pediculosis (head lice) both in its elementary schools and in several daycare centres. Although the number of cases in your centres has been small, there have been cases in every centre, and you are concerned that if staff and parents are not watchful, you may have a serious problem.

    a. Write a memo to the supervisors and staff of each centre advising them of what to look for and which procedures to follow if head lice are found. (See Chapter 3 for memo format.)

b. Write a letter to parents at each daycare centre, advising them of the potential problem.

1.8 After several cases of severe acute influenza occur in a local hospital, Seniors' Independent Living Centre, a retirement home for which you work, is taking precautions to prevent a further outbreak. As part of these precautions, there are restrictions on visitors to the facility. Residents may have only one visitor at a time. The main entrance has been closed, and visitors must enter via the emergency entrance, where they will be interviewed and screened before admittance.

a. Write an internal memo to staff explaining the procedures.

b. Write a letter to be sent to residents' families announcing the new policy.

1.9 Your halfway house has received a new resident, a paroled pedophile. The media have publicized the new resident, and your halfway house has been the target of demonstrations by angry neighbours. Last night a rock was thrown, breaking a window, and other minor vandalism occurred.

a. Write an incident report documenting what happened.

b. Write a memo to staff discussing the incident and follow-up measures.

1.10 See http://www.cjiwr.com/stride.htm for a program for social reintegration inside prison for female prisoners.

a. You would like to introduce this program in a local women's facility. Write a memo to prison staff explaining the program.

b. Announce the program to possible participants.

c. Write a letter to potential sponsors asking for donations of materials to be used in the program.

1.11 The social reintegration program from Exploration 1.10 has been in operation for a year and a half. A participant has had an idea: to sell arts and crafts created in the program and donate the funds raised to local women's shelters.

a. Write a letter to local stores asking for participation (i.e., space to sell the arts and crafts).

b. Advertise the arts and crafts to the local community.

c. Write a letter to potential sponsors for materials to create these arts and crafts.

CHAPTER 2

A BRIEF INTRODUCTION TO THE PERSONAL INFORMATION PROTECTION AND ELECTRONIC DOCUMENTS ACT (PIPEDA)

Overview: An understanding of PIPEDA is crucial for all workers in Canada. This chapter provides an introduction to the Act and to some practical issues for human services workers.

Human services workers have traditionally been concerned about their clients' confidentiality. Professional standards of practise have emphasized care for a client's privacy. Canadian legislation has now caught up with everyday practise in the human services field.

The Personal Information Protection and Electronic Documents Act (PIPEDA) became law on January 1, 2004. PIPEDA covers all organizations that collect, use, or disclose personal information in the course of commercial activities in most provinces across Canada. Quebec, Alberta, and British Columbia have their own privacy legislation that is felt to be substantially similar to PIPEDA, and so those provinces are not covered by PIPEDA. Ontario health information is covered under "substantially similar" provincial legislation, while PIPEDA covers all other sectors. As of the writing of this text, all other provinces are governed by PIPEDA.

PIPEDA protects a person's personal information, regardless of the format in which that information exists—print, audio, electronic, digital, and so on.

WHAT IS PERSONAL INFORMATION?

Personal information, according to PIPEDA, is any factual (data) or subjective (e.g., judgments) information about an identifiable individual, whether recorded or not. Verbal statements are therefore covered by PIPEDA.

Personal information could include a person's name, gender, age, height, weight, or other physical characteristics, as well as any judgments or diagnoses made concerning that individual. Personal information includes a person's credit record, medical record, and intentions (for example, the fact that a person has applied for a different job is considered personal information and is covered by the Act).

WHAT ISN'T PERSONAL INFORMATION?

The fact that a person works at a particular organization, along with that person's title, business address, and telephone number, is not considered personal information.

Within an organization, employee information such as office and e-mail addresses are not covered under the Act.

PIPEDA'S 10 PRINCIPLES

PIPEDA sets out 10 principles for the collection, use, and disclosure of personal information. All organizations are legally responsible for ensuring that their employees follow these 10 principles.

1. Accountability

   All organizations, no matter how small, must appoint a privacy officer who oversees PIPEDA compliance. In many human services agencies there is no full-time privacy officer; rather, someone in the agency has that designation and responsibility in addition to his or her other duties.

   The privacy officer is the point person who ensures that the organization protects all personal information, including information transferred to third parties. This means that even when the information leaves the organization, the responsibility for its safekeeping doesn't end. For example, when referrals are made to another professional, the agency must be sure that, before the information is transferred, the professional receiving the information complies with PIPEDA guidelines.

   The organization is also required to develop and implement a privacy policy that is PIPEDA-compliant. Employees must be trained on the policy and supported in applying the policy in their daily work. The day-to-day operations of an organization must not be in conflict with PIPEDA requirements.

2. Identifying Purposes

   Before personal information of any kind is collected, the organization is expected to identify why that information is needed and how it will be used. An organization needs to document why the information is collected, and when it collects the information the agency must inform the individual to whom that information belongs why the information is needed. After getting the person's consent (see below), if the use of the information changes, that new purpose must be identified and consent gained before the information can be used for that different purpose.

3. Consent

   Consent must be obtained from any person from whom or about whom personal information is collected. To obtain consent, an organization is required to inform the person "in a meaningful way" of the purposes of collecting this data, how it will be used, and who will have access to it (purpose, use, and disclosure). "In a meaningful way" means that the organization needs to ask for consent in a way that the individual can understand. The way in which this is done may vary according to the individual's needs. The language may need to be simplified and the idea of consent explained simply. In some cases, consent may need to be requested through a translator to ensure that the individual fully understands.

Consent must be given willingly, without the use of threats or coercion. However, there are cases where consent is a condition of being served. For example, if an individual chooses not to share personal information that is required to determine if she or he is eligible for a service (for instance, age or financial status, when relevant), it is not considered a threat to make it clear that the individual will not be served unless consent is given. If a person is going to receive any sort of therapeutic intervention or counselling, the sharing of personal information is necessary for the person to be helped, so requiring consent is not considered coercion.

4. Limiting Collection
   There must always be a reason to collect personal information. "Because we've always done it" is not much of an answer under the Act. An organization must collect only information that is relevant and must be able to clearly express why that information is needed.

5. Limiting Use, Disclosure, and Retention
   Obviously, personal information can be used only for the purposes for which it was collected and can be disclosed only as identified when consent was made. In addition, personal information should not be kept forever. An organization must destroy personal information when it is no longer needed.

   An organization must have policies, guidelines, and procedures in place to ensure that personal information is kept for a reasonable time period and only so long as it is needed, and destroyed in a secure manner. For example, print documents should be shredded, not simply put in the trash or recycling bin.

An organization needs to determine in a rational way what should be retained, where, and in what form. For example, colleges would keep student grade records in secure storage in the registrar's office without ever destroying them, but the records individual teachers had of student grades would be destroyed when no longer relevant to the teacher—most likely after the students had completed a course and any academic appeals deadline had passed.

6. Accuracy
This guideline is pure common sense. An organization must ensure that the personal information it has is accurate and must update that information when needed.

7. Safeguards
An organization must protect the personal information it has collected against loss or theft and ensure that it is safe from unauthorized access, disclosure, copying, use, or modification. For this reason, some organizations keep electronic documents as PDFs, a format that is more secure than simple document formats.

In practise, this guideline means that employees must keep personal information secure by locking their filing cabinets, protecting their computers with passwords, using those passwords, ensuring that no personal information is left visible when they leave their desks, following secure faxing procedures, and so on. When speaking on the phone, they need to be sensitive to the possibility of confidential information being overhead.

8. Openness
Organizations need to let people know that they have a privacy policy. Privacy policies must be written in clear,

understandable language and be easily accessible. Most organizations post their privacy policy on their website.

9. Individual Access

Essentially an individual's personal information belongs to that person. An organization is given the right to collect and hold on to it for a reasonable space of time, but the true owner of the information is always the individual. Therefore, people have a right to access their personal information held by an organization. An individual can request that an organization explain the use to which the information has been put and provide a list of organizations to which the information has been provided. Since the use and disclosure need to have been made with the individual's consent, nothing should come as a surprise when the person receives access.

Finally, a person has the right to correct any inaccurate information there might be in his or her file.

10. Challenging Compliance

An organization is required to develop simple, easily accessible complaint procedures for when an individual feels the organization has not complied with PIPEDA guidelines. Complainants must be informed of what they can do to pursue their complaint, both through the organization's complaint process and through the provincial and federal privacy complaint process.

An organization must investigate all complaints, even if they seem frivolous or unfounded. Should an organization find problems with its PIPEDA compliance, the organization must correct any shortcomings in its policies and practices regarding personal information.

Finally, it is an offence under the Act to destroy any information a person has requested, to retaliate against an employee who has identified an issue to the privacy commissioner or has refused to violate PIPEDA when directed to by someone in the organization, or to obstruct any PIPEDA investigation.

EXEMPTIONS TO PIPEDA REQUIREMENTS

Exemptions to the PIPEDA requirements do exist that are relevant to human services workers. For example, personal information can be collected if it is clearly in the individual's best interests and consent cannot be obtained in a timely fashion; personal information can be used without consent in an emergency situation; and personal information can be disclosed without consent if required by law. This last situation is especially relevant in the human services field. If a worker suspects child abuse, legislation requires him or her to report that suspicion. Some but not all provinces require workers to report suspected elder abuse. Danger to public safety or perceived threats of violence to others or to the client's own person would be reported without consent. Safety overrides privacy considerations.

WHERE TO FIND OUT MORE

The Privacy Commissioner of Canada has a website, http:// www. priv.gc.ca, which includes an extensive amount of information on PIPEDA. One recent area of interest is the impact of social networking on privacy. Take a look at http://www.priv. gc.ca/speech/2010/sp-d_20100512_ed_e.cfm for a discussion of this subject.

EXPLORATIONS

2.1 You are the privacy officer for your organization. Write a memo to staff outlining what they should do regarding their personal workspace (e.g., desk, filing cabinets) and their use of technology (e.g., computer, phone, fax machine) to ensure they are in compliance with PIPEDA.

2.2 Consent must be obtained in a meaningful way from an individual. Design an adolescent-friendly consent form.

2.3 Many organizations post their privacy policies on their websites. Go to the website of an organization in your field, download their privacy policy, and note how it conforms to the PIPEDA guidelines.

2.4 Complete the privacy quiz at http://www.priv.gc.ca/quiz/index_e.cfm to test your understanding of this topic.

2.5 Write a memo to staff advising them of acceptable and unacceptable uses of social networking in your workplace.

CHAPTER 3

MEMOS, E-MAILS, AND LETTERS

Overview: This chapter provides a brief introduction to memo, e-mail, and letter conventions.

As a general rule, memos are sent within the organization and letters go outside. The major exception to this rule is actually not an exception at all. When someone is terminated, that person is given a termination *letter* rather than a memo. However, at the moment of termination the person is no longer part of the organization, so the rule still holds: memo in, letter out. E-mails can be sent either externally or internally, and so they share the structural features of both letters and memos.

E-mails are usually signed, often using the "signature" feature of the organization's e-mail program. E-mails can be formal or informal, depending on the audience and context. They can have the informality of instant messaging, can be the equivalent of an electronic memo, or can be quite formal, with attachments, charts, and so on. Consider the audience and context when choosing your approach.

Structurally, there are two approaches in organizing either a memo, e-mail, or letter. The writer can use either a direct or an indirect approach. A direct approach is used when the audience for the communication will be positive or indifferent about what you are writing. An indirect approach is used when the audience response will likely not be favourable (you're delivering bad news) or if the reader must be persuaded (as with a request or suggestion).

With a direct approach, you get right to the point immediately: open with what you want (the letter's purpose), give the necessary details, then close with the next steps (what you want the reader to do). Here's an e-mail using the direct approach.

```
To:      Distribution list
From:    Sheila Strachan
Subject: Holiday party
Date:    November 20, 2011

December is almost here, and the agency is planning
our annual holiday party. We all had a great time
last year and look forward to another enjoyable get-
together. The party committee is grateful for every-
one's extensive feedback on last year's gathering,
and this year's will incorporate your suggestions.
For the first time ever, we'll have the party off-
site. Here are all the details:

Date:  December 20, 2011
Time:  7:00-12:00 p.m.
Place: Archway Dining Lounge
       2047 Renforth Drive
       (see map attached)

Dress:       Semi-formal
Cost:        Free for staff members; $20 for guests
Activities:  Dinner, dancing (DJ), cash bar, door
             prizes

If you plan to attend, please RSVP to Cindy George
(ext. 237) by December 10. Please let her know if
you or your guests have any dietary requirements.
Payment for guest tickets must be received by
December 15; Cindy is handling ticket sales.

Hope to see everybody there, so we can party hearty!

Sheila Strachan
Area Director
Roy McMillen Foundation
sstrachan@roymcmillen.ca
```

Everyone loves a party, and the planning for this year's holiday party took into account people's feedback, so you would assume that people getting this e-mail would be positively disposed. You therefore can get right to the point, give people the details they need, and be done.

Here's an example of a letter using the direct approach, generated by a group of students.

Father John Redmond Secondary School
30 Valermo Drive
Toronto, Ontario
M8Z 1Y4
416-253-1234

February 3, 2011

Constable Jerry Brown
51 Division
Metropolitan Toronto Police Force
3 Jane Street
Toronto, Ontario
M2K 1P3

Dear Constable Brown:

I am the president of the Father John Redmond Parent Council, and I would like to invite you to speak at our March School Council meeting.

The School Council meeting will focus on a discussion of whether we should begin a peer mediation program at our school. Other schools with peer mediation programs have recommended we have you in to speak about setting up a peer mediation program.

Date: March 15, 2011
Time: 7:30 p.m.
Location: Father John Redmond School cafeteria, 30
          Valermo Drive

Could you address an audience of about 30–35 parents on your experiences setting up peer mediation programs? We are especially interested in hearing about

(continued)

- the process for setting up a program.
- the challenges of running a program.
- the results programs have shown.

The presentation should be approximately 15 minutes, with a further 15 minutes for questions.

Please let me know by February 25 if you'll be able to address our group, so I can advertise your presentation. Thank you.

Sincerely,

Lucy Valentino

Lucy Valentino
President
Father John Redmond Parent Council

The students assumed that the reader, Constable Brown, would be positively disposed toward the request, since he is a community liaison officer. They therefore chose the direct approach. Constable Brown's reply would either use the direct approach, if he's able to accept the invitation, or the indirect approach, if he's unable to attend the meeting. Here is an example of the former, again student-generated, followed by the negative response. Note the differences in how the two letters are structured.

Metropolitan Toronto Police Department
51 Division
3 Jane Street
Toronto, Ontario
M2K 1P3

February 7, 2011

Lucy Valentino
President, Parent Council
Father John Redmond High School
30 Valermo Drive
Toronto, Ontario
M8Z 1Y4

Dear Ms. Valentino:

Thank you for the invitation to address your March meeting. I'd be happy to accept. I'd like to confirm the details of the presentation:

Date: March 15, 2011
Time: 7:30 p.m.
Location: Father John Redmond High School cafeteria,
           30 Valermo Drive

I'll deliver a 15-minute presentation on peer mediation programs to an audience of 30–35 parents, with 15 minutes for questions. I will cover

- the process for setting up a peer mediation program.

- the challenges running a program.

- the results of programs I've helped set up.

I will require a computer and screen or laptop hookup for the presentation. I have enclosed a copy of the handout I'll be distributing that night. I'll be bringing 40 copies; please let me know if more will be needed.

If you need to contact me, please call me at 416-274-7788, ext. 421, or e-mail me at jbrown@mtpd.com. Once again, thanks for your invitation. I look forward to working with your group.

Sincerely,

Jerry Brown

Jerry Brown
Constable, Badge #423

Enclosure

Metropolitan Toronto Police Department
51 Division
3 Jane Street
Toronto, Ontario
M2K 1P3

(*continued*)

February 7, 2011

Lucy Valentino
President, Parent Council
Father John Redmond High School
22 Valermo Drive
Toronto, Ontario
M8Z 1Y4

Dear Ms. Valentino:

Thank you for your invitation to speak about peer mediation programs at your March School Council meeting. Peer mediation programs are an effective way to decrease violence in schools and help students learn strategies for conflict resolution.

Unfortunately, I have another speaking engagement on March 15. I'd like to present two alternatives:

- Constable Fred Jones could address your group in my place. Constable Jones has worked with me on a number of peer mediation projects.
- I am available to speak at your April meeting, if the talk can be rescheduled.

Please let me know if either option works for your group and, if so, which you prefer. We look forward to helping your group decide if a peer mediation program is right for your school.

If you would like to contact me by phone, I can be reached at 416-274-7788, ext. 421, between 9:00 a.m. and 6:00 p.m. most days, or by e-mail at jbrown@mtpd.com. I look forward to hearing from you.

Sincerely,

Jerry Brown

Jerry Brown
Constable, Badge #423

An indirect approach builds to the main point. In this example, Constable Brown begins by thanking the group for the invitation and acknowledging the importance of the topic. He moves on to give the bad news that he is unavailable to speak, but offers positive options and closes in a forward-looking way.

In all of these examples, note the use of bulleted lists to make ideas easier for the reader to grasp. In memo and letter writing, you want to use reader-friendly prose. Think about using bulleted or numbered lists, italics and boldface, or even subheadings to help the reader catch your message easily.

E-MAIL GUIDELINES

Here are some e-mail guidelines:

- Always proofread your e-mails meticulously. Perhaps because the writer doesn't usually print a hard copy of an e-mail before sending, e-mails seem especially vulnerable to typos and misspellings.
- Be conscious of the difference between instant messaging and on-the-job e-mails. Business e-mails, even when relatively informal, are not the same as instant messaging. It is never appropriate to use instant-messaging short forms (e.g., LOL [laughing out loud] or BTW [by the way]). In the same way, emoticons (e.g., ☺) are not considered appropriate in even the most informal business communication.
- Be brief, but be clear. Don't sacrifice clarity for conciseness. Being concise does not mean using only a few words; rather, it means using just enough words to get your message across successfully—no more and no less. As an aunt of mine used to say, an elegant sufficiency.
- Be aware that an e-mail is a lasting record. E-mails might look like instant messaging, but they live forever on an organization's computer system.
- In the same way, be aware that e-mails can be forwarded. Don't say anything you don't want the whole agency to see. There are commands in every e-mail system to block forwarding—use them when appropriate.

- Use e-mail etiquette:

  - Most people are aware that using all capital letters is SHOUTING and RUDE, so don't do it.
  - Don't "reply to all" on messages unless your reply really is relevant to everyone who will get it—it often isn't. People hate to get every little response to something sent out to an e-mail distribution list. It drives them INSANE, so, again, don't do it.

Finally, improper use of e-mail may be the most common way for workers to breach confidentiality. E-mails don't disappear into the ether—they move on to have a life of their own, so beware.

SUMMARY

FORMAT FOR MEMO WRITING

```
To:       Human services students
From:     Lucy Valentino
Subject:  Format for memo writing
Date:     August 15, 2011

Memos do not usually include a salutation ("Dear
Students")—the "To" line accomplishes that function.
However, you can use the recipient's first name if
you want to create a casual feel for your memo and
if your relationship with the recipient justifies
using his or her first name.

All paragraphs in a memo begin at the margin (no
indentation). Memos are single-spaced, with double
spacing between paragraphs. Sentences should be
short, minimizing wordiness. Indented point-form
lists are useful for some purposes.

Memos are not usually signed. Some organizations do
require signatures, but that is not common practice.

Remember your reader. Meet his or her needs. Write
clearly, tactfully, forcefully. Use the active
voice. Don't—repeat, DON'T—forget to proofread!
```

FORMAT FOR LETTER WRITING

27 Milcroft Dr.
Willowdale, Ontario M2S 5T6

August 15, 2011

Human Services Students
Humber College
Lakeshore Campus
Toronto, Ontario M4C 6T9

Dear Students:

This letter is written in full block format. Although there are other formats for letter writing, full block is the format most popular in business and the professional world today.

As you can see, everything begins at the margin; nothing is indented. A letter written in full block format is much easier to type than one written in any of the other formats. That is probably the main reason for its popularity.

You will also note that the paragraphs are single-spaced; double spacing occurs between paragraphs. Paragraphs should be brief. Get to the point; don't clutter your prose with deadwood. Think of your reader. Meet his or her needs.

Although it is important to be efficient, do not alienate your reader by being too abrupt. Remember that you are writing to a human being who needs to hear your voice. Speak to your audience clearly, simply, and effectively.

Sincerely,

Lucy Valentino

Lucy Valentino
Professor, English

EXPLORATIONS

3.1 A long-time agency employee is retiring. Write an e-mail to staff members announcing a surprise retirement lunch for this individual.

3.2 Your agency has a policy of allowing flextime (i.e., staff can determine their own starting and ending times, which do not need to be exactly the same each day, so long as they put in the requisite number of hours per week). For the most part, the flextime policy has worked well. However, a few workers have been abusing the policy, which is leading to some bad feelings among the staff. Write an internal memo addressing the situation.

3.3 Write a memo to your supervisor requesting funds to attend a conference in your field. Go to a website for a professional organization in your field, such as http://www.oacyc.org, for announcements of upcoming or past conferences so your memo can be realistic.

3.4 You are a supervisor in your organization/agency. Write a memo to all staff announcing a mandatory training session on PIPEDA and its impact on the organization's policies and procedures. (*Note: You are aware that some staff are already grumbling about the extra work they feel PIPEDA compliance will cause.*)

3.5 Your organization/agency will be moving next month to a new location. In the old location, parking was free for staff. In the new location, you are in a larger building with several occupants. There will be a fee for parking because the agency will be charged for parking lot use. Write a memo announcing the new parking policy and procedures for staff to obtain a pass to access the parking lot.

3.6 You have been working at an organization/agency for nine months. You are getting married next summer and would like to go to Europe for three weeks on your honeymoon. However, at that time you will be entitled to only two weeks' vacation. Furthermore, the organization has a policy of not allowing staff to take more than two weeks off during the summer, since that is the most desirable vacation season. Write a memo requesting the three weeks off, two as paid vacation and one as unpaid leave.

3.7 An employee has requested permission to attend an annual conference in the field. He has also requested that the agency pay his conference fee, travel, and accommodation. The conference and expenses have been covered in the past and time off has been granted, but unfortunately this year one staff member who would normally cover that employee's duties while he was at the conference will be away recovering from surgery. The other staff member who could fill in will be out of town at the time of the conference, attending her parents' 50th anniversary celebration. Write an e-mail refusing the employee's request.

3.8 As a representative of students in your program, write a letter to a community group (e.g., Lions Club, Knights of Columbus) requesting their support for a campaign to raise awareness of violence against children.

3.9 You have graduated from your college. You have been asked for a monetary donation to be put toward student scholarships. You do not have available cash right now. However, you are willing to help out in other ways. Write a letter turning down the cash request but offering another option or options.

3.10 You work at the Ministry of Community and Social Services. You have received an excellent proposal for a program, but you do not have the budget in this fiscal year to provide funding. Write a letter declining funding.

3.11 As a representative of your fellow students, write a letter to the coordinator of your program recommending two or three changes that should be made to your program. Any aspect of the program can be used.

3.12 Write an e-mail after the fact to your teacher in this course, explaining why you missed the midterm or final exam and requesting permission to make up the exam.

3.13 To bolster staff morale, your agency is instituting a reward and recognition program. Write an e-mail to the staff announcing the program.

3.14 Write a letter to the dean of your school suggesting that early morning classes be abolished for students in your program.

3.15 Since beginning at your agency, you have worked a 9:00 a.m. to 5:00 p.m. shift. You now wish to take an evening class at a local college, but would need to be off work by 4:00 p.m. two days a week to do so. Write a memo to your supervisor requesting a change to your work hours so you can take this class.

3.16 You are on a committee that is putting together a conference for college students on emerging trends in your field.

    a. Write a letter requesting sponsor support.

    b. Write a letter to a potential conference speaker inviting that person to present a workshop session or the keynote address.

    c. Advertise the conference via e-mail to your college community.

3.17 Your job involves considerable travel between group homes or schools, so you spend a fair amount of time in transit between locations. Write a memo to your director requesting approval to purchase a digital voice recorder so you can be productive while on the road.

3.18 You have been asked to deliver the keynote speech at a Community and Social Services conference being held at your college. Write a letter accepting the invitation.

3.19 You are concerned about the potential impact of employees' use of social networking sites on the image of your agency. Write an e-mail to staff presenting the issue and providing guidelines for appropriate use of social networking sites.

3.20 You are an employee who received the e-mail in Exploration 3.19, and you are not happy because you feel that the agency has no business trying to legislate your private life. Write an e-mail response.

3.21 You have received the e-mail response in Exploration 3.20. Respond to the disgruntled employee.

3.22 Your agency has always sponsored a holiday party. However, times are tough, and the party has been cut from the budget. Send an e-mail to staff letting them know the bad news.

3.23 Write a memo to your supervisor requesting permission to attend one of the training sessions found at http://www.cjiwr.com/revive.htm, http://www.cantraining.org/cti_website_002.htm, or http://www.thtcentre.com/.

3.24 Write a memo to your supervisor requesting an in-house workshop at your organization on Family Group Decision Making (see http://www.cjiwr.com/family-group-decision-making.htm).

3.25 Write an e-mail to staff announcing the workshop in Exploration 3.24.

3.26 You have been asked to organize an activity for the clients at your agency. You have an idea for an activity that will require the use of a larger space, perhaps a gym once a week. Write a letter to the principal of a local high school requesting the use of the gym during a specific time.

3.27 As principal of a local high school, you have received a request from a social agency asking you to allow its clients the use of your high-school gym for an extracurricular activity, one evening each week. You would like to support the organization, but at present the gym is in constant use during the hours that have been requested. Deny the request.

3.28 Write a letter to your local MPP advocating that prisoners be given the right to vote (see http://www.johnhoward.ca).

3.29 The car you normally use to go from group home to group home (or school to school) broke down yesterday. This car isn't a company car; you own it. Write a memo to your supervisor asking for funds for a rental car so that you can continue to work. You also need to ask for permission to use the car for personal use while yours is being fixed.

3.30 The staff room in your agency is a place where most people eat their lunches. Lately, you have noticed that some people are not cleaning up after they finish eating, leaving dirty dishes, glasses, and garbage behind. Write a memo to be posted requesting that staff keep the room clean.

3.31 The annual holiday party is approaching, and you are in charge of inviting staff. For this year's holiday party, you are requesting staff to contribute food because it is a potluck. Write a memo inviting staff to the party. You also want to mention that you are taking donations for a local homeless shelter at the party.

3.32 Your agency just bought new computers, and you want to donate the old computers to a new agency. Write a letter to this new agency explaining that you are willing to donate the old computers to help jumpstart their agency. The computers still work well, but they are an older make.

3.33 You work at a nursing home that has a unit for seniors with Alzheimer's disease and other dementias. You have heard about an idea that some nursing homes have tried with female dementia patients. They have provided dolls for these patients to care for.

  a. Write a memo suggesting that the unit implement this idea.
  b. Write a letter to the patients' families about this initiative.

3.34 The business next door to your agency plays loud music periodically during the day. This music is interrupting the work of staff and is upsetting some clients. Write a letter to the business asking them to turn their music down. Remember to keep goodwill.

3.35 Your group home is having its annual holiday party. Write a letter to the parents of clients in the home inviting them to the party.

The following explorations might also be expanded into funding proposals or formal reports:

3.36 Write a letter to the Minister of Corrections advocating that the community chaplain program be reinstated (see http://www.johnhoward.ca).

3.37 Write a memo to your supervisor suggesting that your organization provide appropriate job-search clothing to released prisoners.

3.38 Write a memo suggesting that your organization set up a "big brother" or "big sister" ex-con mentorship program to help released prisoners cope with life outside prison.

3.39 In some correctional institutions, prisoners can work toward post-secondary diplomas or degrees (see http://www.youtube.com/watch?v=hTuGwqRlgBw).

  a. Write a memo suggesting such a program to your institution.
  b. Your institution is interested in starting such a program. Write a letter to a local college or university inviting them to partner in this initiative.

CHAPTER 4

RECORD KEEPING, RECORDING TOOLS, AND SHORT REPORTS IN THE HUMAN SERVICES AGENCY

Overview: The writing you will be doing in the field will entail filling out forms, as well as drafting memos, letters, and short reports. You may even find yourself writing a longer document, such as a funding proposal or a formal report. This chapter briefly discusses record keeping and then moves on to various types of short reports.

RECORD KEEPING

Human services agencies of all kinds keep records of their dealings with clients. To simplify the task, agencies provide forms for some of the routine record keeping. Workers are expected to complete the forms clearly, completely, and accurately.

Workers sometimes complain that record keeping ties up valuable time that they could otherwise devote to their clients. It is true that we sometimes seem to be drowning in a sea of paper, but agency record keeping is a necessary process.

Records track a client from the beginning of service, throughout the service process with the agency, and on to his or her discharge. Good records summarize the essential aspects of a client's case, crystallize goals, define strategies, and illustrate progress in meeting goals. Record keeping, like any form of writing, can be a way to think on paper. Records can help a worker to be proactive, rather than reactive, by requiring the worker to summarize relevant facts, articulate judgments, and formulate goals, as well as to detail strategies for achieving those goals. Records such as review reports allow workers to stand back and assess a client's progress, and perhaps change tactics if the client is not making progress.

Records also allow for continuity of service. Accurate records provide case histories that allow agencies or professionals to more easily assume others' clients should the original staff members leave or become ill. In this way, records allow clients to adjust to new staff without having to start at the beginning of the care process.

BASIC GUIDELINES FOR RECORD KEEPING

As noted in Chapter 2, records are covered by legislation dealing with privacy and an individual's access to information. Remember, a record is defined as almost any form of information, including letters, daily logs, case notes, memos, drawings, digital audio or video recordings, and computer files. Therefore, a record includes *all* agency records, from the most informal to the most formal. All records, no matter how informal, are eligible for subpoena.

What are the implications of all this for the human services worker? Records of all types must be treated with respect. You should never have the attitude, "No one is going to see this anyway, so who cares?" Quite frankly, you never know who will see them. You are responsible for your record keeping. The client has access to his or her records; the client also controls access to those records. (You will notice that in many examples, I mention that I assume the client gave the worker permission to share personal information.)

Here are some basic guidelines for keeping good records. Your agency will no doubt have additional guidelines, but the following are some commonsense rules to keep in mind:

1. Complete your records by word processing or handwriting them legibly. Legible handwriting is a MUST. What good is a daily log entry that no one can read?
2. Include date and time for all reports.

3. Do not use pencil or erasable pen. Records are permanent, so use something that cannot be erased.
4. Do not use ditto marks.
5. Do not erase or use correcting fluid to correct mistakes. Different agencies have their own procedures for correction. Many require that you draw a line through errors and write "error" on that line or initial the error. The point is that erasures or covered-up errors have no place in a legal document, which is what records are.
6. Never sign for someone else. You are responsible for what is recorded under your name.
7. Leave no blank lines. Follow agency procedure by crossing out blank spaces, writing "N/A" (not applicable), and so on. In a record that you have signed, you do not want to leave blank spaces where someone else might add material.
8. Use exact details.
9. Spell correctly, especially when recording medications. Bad spelling destroys professional credibility and in some instances can be very dangerous.
10. No matter how informal the record, never refer derogatively to a client or use inappropriate language.

AGENCY RECORDING FORMS

Students using this text will be studying a variety of fields, from Child and Youth Work to Early Childhood Education to Developmental Service Work, etc. The specific recording forms you will use in your career will vary. Your teacher may go into detail on the specific types of recording tools you are likely to be using in the future. I will focus on some general principles of good recording forms. A good recording form helps a worker; it doesn't get in the way. What do I mean by that? If it takes a worker more time to figure out a form than to use it, something is wrong. It should be clear to a worker what the form is asking for and why.

The "why" is important. An agency shouldn't drown in a sea of paper (or computer files). Especially in this computer age, it seems so easy to generate documents—and more documents—and more. It is essential that an agency focus on the purpose of a record. Is this record necessary? Why? How can it be made "user-friendly"? An agency needs to do this not only for practical survival purposes ("Worker Crushed by Paper Load") but also as a legal necessity. Remember the PIPEDA guidelines. Anything that is documented must have been documented for a reason, a reason that can be rationally explained (not just "We always filled in this form before...").

Refer to pages 41 and 42 for two examples, based on actual recording tools, of agency forms to report an incident or serious occurrence. Notice how very different they are. Which do you think would be easier to work with?

INCIDENT REPORT

Client Name _____

Type of Incident _____

Date of Incident _____

Time _____

Give brief description of incident (include precipi-
tating factors):

_____

_____

_____

_____

Action taken:

_____

_____

_____

_____

Further action advised:

_____

_____

_____

Signature of staff member

_____

Signature of supervisor

INCIDENT REPORT

Date of Incident _____ Time _____

Place _____

Name of person reporting _____

Name(s) of person(s) involved _____

Describe what precipitated the incident _____

_____

_____

Describe the sequence of events _____

_____

_____

What action was taken in response to the incident?

_____

_____

_____

Who else was present? _____

_____

_____

Who was informed? _____

When? _____ By whom? _____

What follow-up is necessary? _____

_____

_____

Signature _____

Date _____ Time _____

SHORT REPORTS

Not all circumstances are covered by standard agency forms. Often, human service professionals must work their way through a writing task. Consider the following situation.

INVESTIGATION REPORT

You are the director of a recreational day program for senior citizens. On October 13 you have a rash of absences from the program. Of the 50 seniors who normally attend the program, only 15 show up that morning. You begin to call your clients' families, and you discover that the clients share similar symptoms: diarrhea and intestinal upset. In fact, 10 of the seniors experienced symptoms so severe that family members have taken them to the emergency department of the local hospital. You contact the hospital and are told the tentative diagnosis: salmonella poisoning. The diagnosis will not be final until the stool-sample test results are in, but the doctor in charge feels fairly confident that it is correct.

If the diagnosis is confirmed, the hospital is required to notify the Public Health Department. Because the 35 affected seniors all attend your program, you know that the public health officer will soon be contacting you. So you decide to investigate how this salmonella outbreak could have occurred.

You begin by finding out everything you can about salmonella. You learn that salmonella enteritis is a type of food poisoning caused by eating foods contaminated with salmonella bacteria. The most common sources are undercooked poultry and contaminated dairy products, such as eggs and cheese. You learn that heat destroys salmonella bacteria.

You look back over the menus of the past few days. The centre served chicken salad sandwiches three days ago, but the chicken had been boiled so that a portion could be used in chicken soup the following day. Any salmonella bacteria that might have been present were destroyed through boiling.

You notice that deviled eggs were served two days ago, as a side dish with the soup. But deviled eggs are first hard-boiled, so you eliminate the eggs as a possibility.

The afternoon snack two days ago was raw vegetables and cheese cubes. This seems a likely culprit for the contamination. You ask the seniors at the centre today, those who didn't get ill, whether they had eaten the cheese. Although they had eaten the vegetables, not one of them remembered eating any of the cheese. You discover that there is still a small portion of cheese in the refrigerator and send it off to be analyzed.

A week later the lab report on the cheese comes back, confirming salmonella contamination. By now you have been contacted by Carlos Merlino, Public Health Officer, so you sit down to write an *investigation report* to Mr. Merlino. How would you go about doing this?

Actually, you've done the hardest part already. You know what caused the salmonella outbreak. Now you simply have to share what you have learned.

Let's think about how you would do this. What should you include in your report?

First of all, you need to write a *brief summary* to let Mr. Merlino know the topic of your letter. Then you might discuss the *process of your investigation*—what you looked for and how you isolated the culprit. This would be followed by a discussion of the *outcome of your investigation*—what you did when you discovered the source of the poisoning and how those clients who fell ill are doing now.

Why would you write the report in this way? Look at the situation from Carlos Merlino's point of view. What does he want to know? He wants enough information at the outset to be able to understand your letter. He needs to know that you have identified the cause of the contamination correctly— that you have examined all possibilities and have eliminated all but the true source of poisoning. Finally, he needs to know what you did with the results of your investigation and whether the affected clients are now recovered. And he needs to read all this information in a report that is concise and easy to grasp.

Your report might look something like the one below.

INVESTIGATION REPORT

Brookfield Seniors' Centre
453 Murray Avenue
Kamloops, B.C.

October 20, 2011

Mr. Carlos Merlino
Public Health Officer
5645 Regis Way
Kamloops, B.C.

Dear Mr. Merlino:

On October 13, 2011, 35 clients of the Brookfield Seniors' Centre exhibited symptoms of salmonella poisoning. I immediately investigated the cause of the outbreak, and I have traced the infection to contaminated cheese served on October 11 at the Centre.

After Dr. Leslie Phillips of Reading Memorial Hospital informed me of her diagnosis of salmonella poisoning, I reviewed the Centre's menu for the previous week. I was looking for poultry or dairy items that might have contained the bacteria. I discovered three possible sources: chicken salad at lunch on October 10, deviled eggs at lunch on October 11, and cheese at snack on October 11. Both the chicken and the eggs had been boiled, thus killing any potential salmonella bacteria. The cheese, however, had merely been cut into cubes and was not processed in any way.

A piece of leftover cheese was still in our refrigerator, and I sent it to Stanley Laboratories on October 13 to be analyzed. The lab report, dated October 20, confirms that the cheese is contaminated with salmonella bacteria.

We receive a twice-weekly shipment of milk, cheese, and eggs from Hafner's Dairy, here in Kamloops. All dairy products are immediately refrigerated upon receipt, so the contamination is unlikely to have occurred at the Centre. I phoned Bob Hafner on October 20 and informed him of the outbreak. He

(continued)

traced the batch to which the contaminated cheese belonged and tested another block from that batch. It, too, was contaminated with salmonella. Mr. Hafner will be contacting you; he has assured me that he is recalling the balance of that batch of cheese and is investigating how the contamination occurred.

Our affected clients are slowly recovering. There should be no permanent effects, since they received prompt medical attention.

Sincerely,

Theresa Nolan

Theresa Nolan
Director

INSPECTION REPORT

Let's look at another situation.

You are the director of Hartwood Group Home, a residence for 10 boys aged 8 to 12. This residence is part of a larger agency, Beauville Homes.

You and your staff have felt for some time that the present residence is inadequate, and you have finally convinced the board of directors of Beauville Homes to authorize the purchase of a new location for the residence. You are not personally involved in seeking out another house, since you do not have the time to spare from your other duties; however, you will be inspecting any property that is under serious consideration.

You get a call from head office: the agency is ready to put in an offer on a house recommended by the realtor. You are to inspect the property and advise head office on whether to go ahead with the offer to purchase.

What would you include in this report?

First of all, a reminder about format. Unlike the last example, which was written in *letter format*, this report would be written as a *memo*, since it is to remain within the agency. Letters go outside an organization; memos remain inside. (It is actually most likely to be submitted by e-mail, but we will use memo format in this example.)

So what would you include in your memo? What would the person at head office handling this matter most want to know? He or she would likely want to know, up front, whether or not you are recommending the purchase. So begin with your recommendation.

What next? A little background would be helpful. When did you view the property? Which property is it? (You might be writing more than one report.) Was anyone with you?

Now describe the property itself. What is it like in general? What is its overall condition? How many rooms are there? Is there a yard? Is it close to schools? And so on.

Then to the nitty-gritty. What's wrong with it? No property is perfect. What would need to be changed or repaired? Or, if you are recommending not buying, what are the defects or deficiencies that influenced your decision?

Based on the information you're providing, where should the board go from here? Should they put in an offer? Should they put in an offer with conditions (e.g., that the roof be repaired)? Should they put in an offer, and then start looking for a contractor to carry out renovations? Should they forget this property and keep looking?

The actual inspection report might look like the one on page 48.

(Note: Personal information about the sellers of the property is relevant in this report because the agency may be able to get the property at a lower price, given the situation. In another context, personal information like this is simply gossip and would not be included.)

INSPECTION REPORT

To: Mei Li Chin
From: Claudette Brion
Subject: Inspection of 473 Derry Road
Date: Nov. 12, 2010

I recommend that Beauville Homes purchase the house at 473 Derry Road as a new site for Hartwood Group Home.

On Nov. 11, 2010, Jakub Dzielga and I inspected the above property. Hartwood Group Home has been in need of a larger location for some time.

473 Derry Road is a large, five-bedroom, three-bath home with a fenced yard, which backs onto Hydro land. It is two blocks from a public school and three blocks from a municipal park with baseball diamond, soccer field, swimming pool, tennis court, and climbing apparatus. Zoning would permit a group home in this area.

The house itself, though spacious, is in disrepair and would require renovations. It is being sold under power of sale, having been owned by a large family that underwent financial difficulties and ultimately a marriage breakup.

The following repairs and renovations would be required:

1. replacement of overloaded fuse panel with circuit breakers and upgrade of electrical service to the home
2. repair and replastering of walls in master bedroom, living room, and kitchen (several large holes)
3. replacement of carpeting throughout the house
4. replacement of door in main bathroom (hole)
5. repair of broken windows in two back bedrooms
6. repainting of all interior walls

Although these renovations appear extensive, the mortgage holder is offering a very attractive price because the house is under power of sale. Even considering the cost of the renovations, this house would be an excellent buy and would meet our needs for years to come.

I recommend that you put in an offer to purchase this property and hire a contractor to do the necessary renovations. Please contact me at ext. 2246 if you need further information.

PROGRESS REPORT

The agency has bought the house you recommended, and Franklin Home Improvements is carrying out renovations. You are scheduled to move in on July 5.

It is June 15, and you get a call from head office. They're wondering if the residence will be ready in time. You are asked to look at the progress being made and then write a report.

You discover, on visiting the property and talking to the contractor, Alan Franklin, that there may be some difficulties with the July 5 deadline. The electricians had been on strike for three weeks in the spring, and although Franklin's electrician is back on the job now, the renovation is two weeks behind schedule. By working overtime, however, the contractors should complete all major work by the deadline.

The problem now is that the carpet layers' union just took a strike vote, the results of which will be released on June 18. New carpets were to be laid on June 23. If the union does go on strike, the carpeting subcontractor Franklin deals with may continue to lay carpet, using nonunion help, but if Franklin allows that, his other unionized employees will walk off the job. You could, however, move in on July 5 and have the carpets installed after the strike is over. Installing the carpets later will be more difficult and quite disruptive, but you do have this option in the event of a strike.

What would this report look like? What are the people at head office most interested in?

They probably want to know two things: (1) Are the renovations on schedule? and (2) Will being behind schedule make a difference in the moving date?

So you would begin with the information that the renovations are not quite on schedule, but that you will move in on the planned date anyway.

Next, the people at head office would probably want to know what's behind schedule. But first it would be useful to summarize what was to be done when, so planned work could come next. After that, you need to summarize the actual work done (which is rarely as much as was planned), then detail the problems that prevented all the planned work from being finished.

The memo would end with future plans, or where you will go from here.

The progress report on the renovations follows.

PROGRESS REPORT

To: Mei Li Chin
From: Claudette Brion
Subject: Progress on Hartwood Group Home II
          Renovations
Date: June 15, 2011

Renovations on Hartwood Group Home II, located at 473 Derry Road, are about two weeks behind schedule; nonetheless, we should be able to move in by the July 5 deadline date.

Beauville Homes took possession of this property in December 2010 as a new location for Hartwood Group Home, which had outgrown its present setting. The house required extensive renovations, including:

1. replacement of overloaded fuse panel with circuit breakers and upgrade of electrical service to the home
2. repair and replastering of walls in master bedroom, living room, and kitchen (several large holes)
3. replacement of carpeting throughout the house
4. replacement of door in main bathroom (hole)
5. repair of broken windows in two back bedrooms
6. repainting of all interior walls

Franklin Home Improvements was contracted to carry out these renovations. As of today, they have completed items 2, 4, and 5. An electricians' strike, from May 4 through May 25, delayed work on item 1. The painting was also delayed until electrical work could be finished. Carpet was scheduled to be laid after the painting was finished.

The electrician is finishing his work. Painting is beginning and will be completed in time for the scheduled carpet laying, on June 23. There may be a problem, however, with the carpet laying. The carpet layers' union has taken a strike vote, the results of which are not yet known. Should they go on strike, it is uncertain when the carpets will be laid. The

contractor, Alan Franklin, will not use nonunion-
ized help; our union would certainly object to this
as well.

We can move in as scheduled on July 5, however,
even without carpeting. Alan Franklin has assured me
that the carpets can be laid as soon as the strike,
if it occurs, is over. He will attempt to minimize
disruption to our residents and staff. Is this solution acceptable?

LETTER OF REFERRAL

Let's look at another writing task. Human service professionals
frequently have to refer clients to other agencies for appropriate help. How do you go about doing this?

First, who is the audience? Another professional. Second,
what is the purpose? To introduce a client to this professional
and obtain the appropriate services for the client.

What does that professional need to be told?

- who is being referred
- why he or she is being referred
- what you expect to be done

The sample letter of referral on page 52 shows one way of
relating this information. As mentioned in Chapter 3, closing
with a thank-you and contact information is often appropriate
in letter writing.

LETTER OF REFERRAL

Children's Hospital
835 Merrit Street East
Winnipeg, Manitoba

August 6, 2011

Ms. Nadita Singh
Oakdale Community Centre
Winnipeg, Manitoba

Dear Ms. Singh:

I am making this referral on behalf of Ms. Kirsten Bradford, a patient in our Gastrointestinal Disease Unit at Children's Hospital. I request that Kirsten be admitted to your Adolescent Art Therapy program.

Kirsten is a 14-year-old girl who was diagnosed with Crohn's disease in June 2009. Her disease has not responded well to medical treatment. She has been admitted to Children's Hospital 18 times over the past two years, sometimes for weeks at a time. She has undergone various drug treatments, including immune suppressants, anti-inflammatories, antibiotics, and corticosteroids, as well as treatments such as nasogastric and intravenous feeding.

I have worked with Kirsten as a child life specialist during her many hospitalizations. Kirsten has a very positive attitude, but she has sometimes been challenged to maintain that positive attitude in the face of another relapse. I have noticed that by taking part in art activities while in the hospital, Kirsten has been able to reduce her stress and increase her ability to cope.

I therefore request that you admit Kirsten to your Adolescent Art Therapy program. Having access to the cathartic release of art on an ongoing basis would help her continue to cope with her disease. I can be reached at 453-4545, ext. 237, if you require further information. Thank you for your consideration.

Yours truly,

George Chiotacos

George Chiotacos
Child Life Worker

SUMMARY

The following structures were used in the model reports in this chapter. These structures were used because they worked in the particular situations; they should not be followed blindly. Use a structure that fits your particular writing situation. Feel free to use these structures as a starting point, but adapt them to your needs.

Investigation Report
Structure:

  I.   Brief summary/background
  II. Process of investigation
  III. Outcome

Inspection Report
Structure:

  I.   Summary (recommendation)
  II. Background
  III. Description of property
  IV. Deficiencies
  V.   Outcome (recommendation)

Progress Report
Structure:

  I.   Summary
  II. Background: planned work
  III. Work done
  IV. Problems
  V.   Outcome

Letter of Referral
Structure:

  I.   Summary
  II. Who is being referred
  III. Why client is being referred
  IV. Conclusion

EXPLORATIONS

Inspection Reports

4.1   You are the supervisor of Sandy Beach Cooperative Daycare Centre. The parent board has asked you to inspect some used outdoor play equipment, which Lynn's Place Daycare Centre is selling. Write an inspection report to be presented at the next parent board meeting.

4.2   Your day centre for seniors has lost its lease because the building in which it is housed is to be sold. Write an inspection report on an alternative location.

4.3   You are the superintendent of an agency that runs a summer camp for children with physical disabilities. For the past 15 years, the camp has taken place on the country estate of an elderly woman, who always donated the use of her property for July and August. The woman died in November, and her heirs have sold the country estate. However, the deceased woman has left a bequest to the agency of another rural property and a modest amount of money to develop it as a camp. Write an inspection report on the property.

4.4   After graduation, you are active in the alumni group for your program. The group has put you in charge of organizing a reunion/conference for program alumni. The reunion/conference will include both social events and workshops on hot issues in your field. The event will be held at your college in July. Write an inspection report on the on-campus venues where the activities can be held.

4.5   You are the supervisor of Our Place (Peel), the only emergency shelter in Peel Region geared to youth. You are looking for a second location, Our Place II, because you were successful in getting funding for a second shelter. Write an inspection report on a possible site.

4.6   You are the supervisor of a child daycare centre and have been asked to inspect a residential property that is being considered for a second site. Go to the Real Estate Board's multiple listing service (mls) for your area (http://www.mls.ca) to select a property to "inspect." Using the property you have found, write an inspection report. Give your teacher a copy of the mls listing with your report.

4.7   Your agency works with females who have been in trouble with the law. The agency has received funding for short-term housing for female ex-offenders with children. Go to the Real Estate Board's multiple listing service for your area (http://www.mls.ca) to select a property to "inspect" as a site for this short-term housing. Using the property you have found, write an inspection report. Give your teacher a copy of the mls listing with your report.

Progress Reports

4.8 Write a progress report to your instructor on your major project for this course.

4.9 You are a recreation officer with the parks and recreation department in your city. You are involved in setting up an adventure playground in an underprivileged area of the city. Write a progress report on the project, which is two-thirds of the way toward completion.

4.10 Your agency, a counselling service for Aboriginal ex-offenders, has just relocated to new premises, which formerly housed a daycare centre. Renovations are currently underway; they could not be completed before your agency moved in, because you needed to be out of your previous site at the same time this site became available. Write a progress report on the renovations.

4.11 Write a progress report on the camp in Exploration 4.3.

4.12 Your agency is setting up a website. Write a progress report to your supervisor on the website development.

4.13 Write a progress report to the alumni board letting them know how the preparations for the reunion/conference in Exploration 4.4 are progressing. The event will be held at your college in July. It is now May.

4.14 Write a progress report on the renovations to the site for Our Place II in Exploration 4.5.

4.15 You are the supervisor of a child daycare centre, and have been overseeing renovations to the property you inspected in Exploration 4.6. Renovations are three weeks behind schedule. Write a progress report.

4.16 Renovations are underway on the property in Exploration 4.7. Your organization is anxious to begin placing clients in this short-term housing. Prepare a progress report.

Investigation Reports

4.17 You are the director of Eastside Group Home, which houses 10 to 12 adolescent boys who have drug-related problems. A stash of cocaine was found by a counsellor. It was hidden in an infrequently used storage cabinet in the basement. The counsellor, Andy Maleczi, discovered the drugs while looking for a missing piece of baseball equipment. Write an investigation report on this situation.

4.18 You are the manager of Wolthan Memorial Arena, site of the divisional hockey playoffs for 15- and 16-year-olds. At playoffs tempers sometimes run high, and this year is no exception. Especially volatile is the relationship between two teams that have a long-standing rivalry, the Cantville Colts and the East Hornsby Raiders. Players from both teams have taken some cheap shots in earlier games in the series, and the referees are having difficulty controlling the championship game. In the third period, a player from Cantville goes down, screaming that he has been hit with a hockey stick behind the knees. The player is unable to stand and appears to have suffered some orthopedic damage. A brawl ensues, with players, coaches, and parents involved. Although no police charges are laid, the hockey association executive committee asks you to file a report so that it may set appropriate sanctions. Write an investigation report on this incident, adding any details you feel are necessary.

4.19 Two staff members have complained to you about each other, each claiming the other is harassing her and creating a poisoned work environment. Write an investigation report about the complaints.

4.20 One of your clients, a young woman who has been in hiding because of being stalked by an abusive ex-boyfriend, has just been hospitalized with injuries from a beating by that boyfriend. There is a possibility that he had been able to find her because of a confidentiality breach in your agency. Write an investigation report to the Ontario Privacy Officer detailing whether or not a PIPEDA breach occurred.

4.21 You are the supervisor of a 15-person department at the Children's Aid Society. Your department has a modest budget for office supplies. There has been a sudden spike in the actual amount the department is spending for office supplies over the past two months. Write an investigation report to your manager on the situation, inventing any details necessary.

4.22 Take a look at the report at the following link: http://www.provincialadvocate.on.ca/documents/en/RMYC%20Report%20Aug%2009%20to%20Feb%2010%20Mar%2029.pdf. Write an investigation report of any ONE allegation in the report.

Letters of Referral

4.23 For the past six months, you have been working with Valerie Sinclair, a developmentally delayed eight-year-old. Write a referral to an audiologist to have Valerie's hearing tested.

4.24 You are an income maintenance officer with a community service agency. You have begun to suspect that one of your clients, Hal Crawley, is illiterate. Refer him to a literacy program.

4.25 You are a child life worker (recreational therapist) at a children's hospital. Over the past year you have been working with an eight-year-old boy with leukemia who has been repeatedly admitted to the hospital. You have become concerned about the boy's twin sister, who is exhibiting infantile behaviour in reaction to her twin's illness. After speaking with the children's mother, you would like to refer the girl to the hospital's anxiety support group. Write the letter of referral.

4.26 You are a staff supervisor at a facility for troubled youth. Yesterday a resident, Marta R., was found after an unsuccessful suicide attempt. Write a letter of referral for her for follow-up counselling.

4.27 You are a counsellor with the employee assistance program in a midsized company. A senior manager approaches you about her executive secretary. After years of excellent work, the secretary has begun to display a pattern of absenteeism that is affecting her work. You were asked to look into the situation and have met with the secretary. With her permission, write a letter referring her for further assistance.

4.28 You are a social worker at St. Joseph's Health Centre. A 72-year-old woman, Angelina Molina, was admitted with a bowel obstruction, which was treated by a combination of bowel rest and medication. She is ready to be discharged but will need nursing care at home. She has Parkinson's disease, diabetes, and high blood pressure. She lives alone and uses a walker to get around. Write a letter of referral to the Victorian Order of Nurses for in-home nursing care for Mrs. Molina.

4.29 You work with a young man who has a mild developmental disability. In recent months he has been exhibiting increased frustration with many areas of his life and has begun to express that frustration in violent ways. Write a letter of referral for him to an anger management program or counsellor.

4.30 You are a social worker who helps to transition prisoners to life outside prison. Write a letter of referral to the short-term housing in Exploration 4.7 for a female prisoner who is to be released seven weeks from now.

4.31 You are a social worker who helps support former prisoners. A recently divorced middle-aged man has contacted you because of his difficulties coping with lack of access to his children following the marriage breakup. Write a letter of referral for him to the program described at the John Howard Society of Durham website: http://www.jhsdurham.on.ca/dads/.

CHAPTER 5

A TERM-LONG WRITING PROJECT: WHERE TO GET IDEAS AND WHAT TO DO

Overview: This chapter describes a term-long writing project, which can be done either individually or collaboratively.

The next four chapters detail two types of major projects, either of which may be undertaken as the major project in your course. Both are "capstone" projects—that is, projects that call upon everything you have learned in the vocational and generic skills portions of your program. They are designed, as it were, to exercise all your muscles in an integrated exercise routine. They are culminating performances of your professional skills.

This chapter describes a funding-proposal project. Professionals in your area of human services may not write funding proposals as part of their normal duties (on the other hand, many do). However, this project is offered because it allows you to practise the communication skills you are learning in this course, as well as to apply the knowledge you have gained about your field through other courses. This exercise synthesizes and integrates your learning. I would emphasize, though, that the project is not meant to give you the skills to write professional proposals. You would probably need an entire course to do that! Rather, the project pulls together many strands of your learning and may, perhaps, illuminate areas for future exploration. Admittedly, it requires a fair amount of work, but it does promise to be interesting to research and write.

Funding proposals are slightly different from the writing we have done so far in one respect. Up to this point, you have determined the structure of your letters, reports, memos, and e-mails based on your purpose and on your understanding of the audience's needs. The funding proposal, however, has a predetermined structure, set by a funding body based on its own determination of its needs. There is less flexibility, then, in a proposal, yet there is great room for creativity, especially in this project.

Funding proposals are usually written in response to a Request for Proposals (RFP) that sets out a structure that must be followed. Proposals are usually scored by a funding body, with points allotted to each required section in order to ensure fairness to all applicants for funding. Not following the required format is like not answering all the questions on a test—a recipe for disaster!

For this proposal, you are asked to consider the entire field of human services and to focus on a need that is presently not being met, or adequately met, by existing agencies. What would you like to see done, done better, or done differently? Is there a client group that you feel is poorly serviced? Is there a type of program that you think should be tried? Is there a service available elsewhere that you feel should be in place in your community? Is there a shortfall in services to a client group that needs to be addressed?

Your proposal will request funding for a project to meet the need you identify. You will state the project's purpose, discuss the current situation, describe staffing and programming, demonstrate community support, and provide a budget.

This undertaking may seem a bit daunting at first, but it's not as bad as it looks. I'll discuss parts of the proposal in more detail later; first, I'd like to talk about where you might find ideas for the project.

WHERE TO GET IDEAS

The best source of ideas is yourself. In the past, my students have looked to their experiences and frustrations to come up with ideas. For example, the author of the sample proposal in Chapter 6, on post-adoption support groups, had herself been involved for many years in foster parenting, and so had first-hand experience of the lack of resources available in her geographic area. Another student came up with the idea for a teen suicide help line when her friend, feeling suicidal, spent hours trying to get through to a counsellor on the city's suicide help line. Another student, with cerebral palsy, developed the idea of a drop-in centre for young adults with disabilities, since he would have liked a chance to socialize and share the support of other physically challenged youths working toward independence. Another student, whose grandmother had finally been institutionalized with Alzheimer's disease after the family's long, unsuccessful struggle to find community supports, proposed funding a day treatment centre for late-stage Alzheimer's patients, which would allow them to remain with their families.

Have you had an experience that demonstrated to you a gap in social services? Think about that unmet need as you choose a project for your proposal.

Another source of ideas is your placement or work experience. Several students who worked with Aboriginal prisoners presented proposals on post-release agencies, based on Native culture and values, to reduce recidivism (re-offending). Others, who worked with battered women and were aware of the extreme shortfall in services in this area, presented proposals for expanding existing services.

Yet another source is knowledge you have gained from other courses. Is there an approach that should be more widely used? Is there something new that should be tried? One pair of students developed the idea of child and youth workers living with the children's families on a short-term basis to help the entire family, rather than removing the child with problem behaviours to a residential program. During the students' research, a professional they interviewed asked if they would accept a referral!

In short, ideas can come from anywhere—from the newspaper or from simply talking to other people. What do you feel needs to be done or could be done better, more widely, or differently? Talk about it, think about it—then present your bit of the solution.

PARTS OF THE PROPOSAL

Your funding proposal will comprise the following sections: title page, purpose, documentation of current situation, design, community content, evaluation, and budget.

TITLE PAGE

The title page for the proposal should include

1. the title of your agency or project.
2. the name of your sponsor, an established agency that would have reviewed your proposal and offered their approval. They would not necessarily be offering you any money, but they would supply a reference, indicating by their sponsorship that they feel your project is viable and valuable. (Your teacher will probably not require that you actually get the sponsorship of an established agency but, rather, will ask that you include on the title page the name of an agency that would make an appropriate sponsor.)
3. information about the contact person (your name, address, and telephone number).

PURPOSE OF PROPOSED PROJECT

This section describes

1. your project's primary goal, stated in one sentence. What one thing do you hope to achieve with this project? If you can express what you hope to achieve with your project in one sentence, you are clear in your own mind about the

project and are therefore ready to present the proposal to others.

2. your project's supporting goals. What else might it achieve? While you have one overarching goal, there will likely be beneficial spillovers. What other good things will also come out of your project?

3. your client group. Who would be eligible for service? It is important to delineate those eligible and those ineligible for service carefully. Does your program cover a specific age group? Those from a specific area of the city? Who is your target group?

4. measurable program results. What results can you expect from implementing this project? How might you measure those results? What concrete, measurable results could you expect if your project were put into place? Funding bodies expect accountability. Funding is generally given for a specified period. Renewal of funding is usually based on the project's having achieved promised results. A funding body is not only interested in *how* you spent the money but also in *what* you accomplished. If you promised a 20-percent reduction in students dropping out of high school but achieved an 18-percent reduction, you may well be asked about that missing 2 percent of students. Anticipating realistic measurable program results is difficult, but it must be done.

DOCUMENTATION OF CURRENT SITUATION

This section is significant in determining whether your communication will be successful. *You must demonstrate a need for your project.* If your readers cannot see a need for your project, they will not approve it, no matter how good the rest of your proposal is. Prove the need.

You might set out to prove that no other agency is presently doing what you propose your agency should do. In this case, you would also have to demonstrate that it should be done. On the other hand, you might set out to prove that what you propose is presently being done, but that the need for the service is greater than the existing agency's capacity to fulfill that need. For example, consider Figure 10.7 on p. 127. In your province, how many shelters for abused women exist? To obtain funding for an additional shelter, you would demonstrate that there are more women needing emergency shelter than these facilities can handle.

The documentation section might include

1. a description of the current situation. What are the needs of your client group? What is presently being done to meet those needs?
2. hard data related to the current situation. An example of hard data would be an analysis of the waiting lists for shelters for battered women in the community ("hard facts").
3. soft data describing the situation. An example of soft data would be an interview with a shelter administrator.

Soft data is useful, but only if it is backed up by hard data. Soft data alone tends not to be very convincing. Three possible sources of hard data to support your documentation section are Statistics Canada reports (http://www.statcan.gc.ca/start-debut-eng.html), municipal websites (for example, http://www.toronto.ca/demographics/index.htm), and police services websites, which often contain crime statistics and environmental scans (http://www.torontopolice.on.ca/publications/files/reports/2009envscan.pdf).

DESIGN

This section provides

1. the number and type of staff providing direct service to clients (i.e., front-line workers).
2. the number and type of administrative staff (managers, supervisors) and support staff (secretaries, janitors).
3. an organizational chart.
4. job descriptions for all positions. If you obtained the funding you were seeking and needed to hire staff, what duties would be listed in the job posting?

5. hiring requirements for all positions, detailing the credentials, background, experience, and qualities each person must have. Again, if you were actually hiring, what would you be looking for in terms of applicants' background?

6. a full description of the program, explaining what you will be doing in this project. This is the portion that allows you to paint a picture of the project for the funder. Another way to think of it is to tell the story of your project. Let the funder visualize what it is that you will be doing with the money if you get it.

The design section allows you to demonstrate to the funder that you can hit the ground running if you are given funding approval. You are showing that you have thought through implementation of the project, that it's not just a nice idea. You are ready to make that idea reality. Tomorrow.

COMMUNITY CONTENT

This section requires a letter from an appropriate person in the community showing that the project has his or her support. Your teacher will probably not require that you obtain a real letter but rather ask that you write one yourself.

EVALUATION

This section describes how your project will be evaluated. It should explain how you will know if what you're doing is effective or needs to be changed and how your project will be accountable, so that the funding body will know if it is getting its money's worth.

This section discusses

1. the criteria you will use to evaluate the program. How will you know if it is a good program? What should you look for? What would be the signs that the program is effective?

2. the process you will use to evaluate the program. What exactly will you do to gather data for evaluation?

3. who will evaluate the program. Will program staff or administrators be responsible for the evaluation, or will the program be evaluated by someone external?
4. how often the program will be evaluated. Will the evaluation be conducted monthly, every six months, once a year, every two years? The frequency of evaluation should make sense within the context of your project. How often should you check that you are meeting the criteria you set?

BUDGET

Get out your calculator. Human services cost money. Now's the time to figure out how much your project will cost.

This budget has two parts: total cost and a cost breakdown.

First, estimate the total cost of your project. Provide the total cost, the amount requested from this government funding body, and the amount you expect to raise from other sources, such as community groups and corporate donors.

Next, break down the parts that make up the total cost, including

1. salaries
2. benefits (assume 14 percent of salaries)
3. staff training and professional development
4. staff travel
5. supplies
6. food costs
7. rent of premises
8. other rental costs (photocopier, phone, etc.)
9. utilities and taxes
10. insurance
11. repairs and maintenance
12. replacements (damaged furniture, outdated computer, etc.)
13. new furnishings and equipment
14. vehicle operations and maintenance
15. advertising and promotion
16. personal needs (if a residence)
17. other (specify)

18. expenditure recoveries (fees collected from project participants)
19. major capital expenditures (purchase of vehicle, computer equipment, etc.)

If your project involves start-up costs (such as purchasing a building, buying furniture, or other one-time costs), separate them from the amount you would require from year to year.

Be realistic about costs. And be sure that your budget breakdown adds up to the total cost of the project. Nothing's worse than actually getting funding and discovering you had an arithmetic error and didn't ask for enough to run the project. (In reality, though, if your accounting is off, you wouldn't get the funding in the first place.)

SUGGESTIONS FOR APPROACHING THIS PROJECT COLLABORATIVELY

The most important suggestion I have to make is that you choose your partner well. Choose someone with whom you can work and who will work as hard as you do.

Brainstorm together the possible needs your project could address. Come to agreement on one need, and then brainstorm ways to meet that need. Do any preliminary research necessary to settle on a final topic.

Once you have some idea of where you are headed, make a list of everything you will need to do before the project is finished. Make your list as detailed as possible. Remember the answer to the old question of how to eat an elephant: one bite at a time. If you list your work in small "bites," you will be well on your way to completing it.

Once you have a complete list (don't forget to add revision, typing, and proofreading), get out a calendar and work backward from the date the assignment is due. Decide on a reasonable division of labour and set realistic deadlines, preferably with a bit of slack for the unexpected. Be sure to leave time for collaborative revision.

Be aware that the proposal does not need to be worked on in order, beginning with the first section and going through to the end. It only needs to be presented in that order, so work in the order that suits you. Remember, writing is a recursive process—a writer will sometimes move back and forth in the text. When writing this text, for example, I did not work straight through from Chapter 1 through 2 through 3, and so on; instead, I wrote the "easiest" chapters first and worked on the harder chapters bite by bite. If you are blocked with one section of the proposal, work on another for a while. It's become a cliché, but the journey of a thousand miles does begin with the first step (and continues step by step until the end is reached).

EXPLORATIONS

5.1   Spend a few days thinking about what your project will be. Write a memo to your teacher discussing what you would like to work on and why.

5.2   Set out a schedule for yourself for the major project. If you will be working collaboratively with someone, discuss and agree on a division of duties. Your teacher may ask you to hand in the schedule and the duty roster.

CHAPTER 6

STUDENT EXAMPLE OF THE TERM-LONG WRITING PROJECT

Overview: This chapter consists of a student example of a funding proposal. Note that not all funding proposals would be done in exactly this way. A writer would follow the guidelines set by the funding agency.

```
THE POST-ADOPTION FAMILY SUPPORT
   AGENCY OF DURHAM REGION

          sponsored by:
       THE DURHAM REGION
     CHILDREN'S AID SOCIETY

         Contact person:
     Mrs. Patricia Caverly
        4052 Mason Street
       Pickering, Ontario
            L2W 5M6
       tel: (905) 987-6543
```

Source: Courtesy of Patricia Caverly

A. PURPOSE OF PROPOSED PROGRAM

1. The primary goal of the proposed Post-Adoption Family Support Agency is to connect families with existing community supports if they experience problems with their adoptive child (children) after the final papers have been signed.

2. The use of volunteers will help people reach out to others in their community. It is possible that this agency will assist in the formation of a Durham Adoptive Parents Support Group.

   This agency would be able to provide support to families and therefore the likelihood of adoption breakdown would decrease.

3. The client group will be any families who have adopted one or more children, who have signed Finalization of Adoption papers, and who live in the Durham Region.

4. The program's results will be measured each year through questionnaires completed by the families and by the comparison of statistics concerning adoption breakdown before and after the two-year trial period. We will be expecting a decrease of about 20 percent in the rate of adoption breakdown over a two-year period.

B. DOCUMENTATION OF CURRENT SITUATION

The Children's Aid Society (CAS) of the Durham Region currently has only three social workers. One worker, the supervisor, is responsible for administrative duties and has little contact with individual families. The remaining two workers have the total responsibility of interviewing prospective adoptive families, completing home studies, and supervising the first six-month probationary period following the placement of a child in an adoptive home. The large geographic area of Durham places further time restraints on these workers as they visit families in their homes. Therefore, workers have very little time to counsel families who have finalized their adoption and who are now experiencing difficulties with their adoptive children. This is further complicated by the fact that these problems may not surface for a year or more after the adoption is finalized; by this time, the staff at the agency may no longer be the same and, therefore, may not know the family or the situation the child has come from. Families in trouble are often reluctant to contact the CAS, as they fear having their children removed from their home.

There are two parent support groups to which Durham families have access. They are Parents Concerned with Adoption (PCA) and the Ontario Federation of Adoptive Parents. Both groups are very informal, and membership fluctuates considerably. The groups are not really based in the Durham Region, and there is no one person who can be contacted at any given time.

Children who are placed by the Durham Region CAS are often scarred from their earlier life experiences. These scars may cause physical, emotional, and educational crises as the children approach various developmental crossroads in their lives. These are long-term concerns that adoptive families often do not understand and are not always prepared to handle. Families and individuals can be destroyed if there is no appropriate support.

C. DESIGN

1. a. Staff providing direct service to clients:
   - one coordinator
   - four full-time area supervisors
   - two part-time area supervisors
   - volunteers as needed and as trained
   b. One full-time secretary

2. Organizational Chart (see Figure 6.1)

Figure 6.1

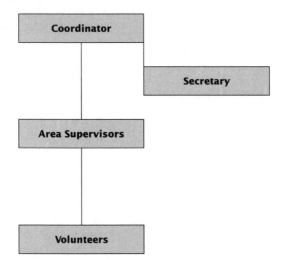

3. Staff Responsibilities and Qualifications

The *coordinator* is responsible for
- handling all initial client intake
- training area supervisors
- obtaining and maintaining resource lists
- attending interagency meetings
- reviewing all questionnaires
- holding monthly meetings and reviewing client plans

The *area supervisor* is responsible for
- recruiting, training, and supervising volunteers
- matching clients with volunteers
- referring clients to other community agencies if this is appropriate
- setting goals with clients
- sending out questionnaires

The *volunteer* is responsible for
- providing one-to-one support for clients
- being reasonably accessible and providing support to his or her client family in non-business hours
- reporting to the area supervisor on a regular basis

The *secretary* is responsible for
- answering the telephone
- typing any necessary correspondence
- taking messages
- compiling statistics
- making appointments for the coordinator

Coordinator
The coordinator should have a B.S.W. and at least two years' experience working with families. Some experience in the field of adoption is considered an asset.

Area Supervisor
Each area supervisor should have an S.S.W. diploma. Ideally, area supervisors will have experience working with families and will have good problem-solving skills. An ability to supervise others will need to be demonstrated.

Volunteers
Volunteers will be individuals and families who have adopted. The agency will hope to be able to access volunteers who have experienced difficult times following adoption and who have shown the ability to commit to their children and to problem-solve. It will be expected that adoptive parent support groups will be of service in helping this agency find volunteers with this type of experience.

Secretary
Good word-processing skills and a pleasant telephone manner will be necessary. Additionally, it is

important that the individual be self-motivated, as the secretary will often be alone in the office.

4. The Program

The Durham Region will be divided into six regions: Ajax-Pickering, Brock, Newcastle, Oshawa-Whitby, Scugog, and Uxbridge. Brock and Scugog will be served by part-time area supervisors for the time being. The remaining four areas will have full-time supervisors. As one of the main goals of this agency is to help people to network and receive support in their own community, the regions have been chosen in such a way that area supervisors, volunteers, and clients can reach one another without incurring long-distance telephone costs. This will encourage families to ask for help and will also be cost-effective for the agency. Because the areas have been chosen with geographic size and easy access to communication—and not population—in mind, it is anticipated that a part-time area supervisor may be needed in both the Ajax-Pickering area and the Oshawa-Whitby area in the future.

Clients will contact the coordinator of the agency initially. He or she, in turn, will conduct an intake interview and then explain the agency's purpose to the family. The family will then be referred to the appropriate area supervisor, who will meet with the family in their home. The family and the area supervisor will discuss the family's concerns, and then the area supervisor will help the family set up a plan. At this point it might be necessary to help the family network with a community organization that can provide specific counselling. The family will be provided with a resource list, and the supervisor will help the family gain access to the appropriate agency. If the family needs to learn specific skills, such as how to deal with the educational system, the supervisor will provide this information. The supervisor will make every effort to team the family with a volunteer family within the community that has experienced a similar problem. As the volunteer family and the client family establish a relationship, the area supervisor will decrease her direct contact with the family. She will continue to provide guidance and resources to the volunteer family as required.

As this program is designed to provide support to adoptive parents and their children, the focus of the program will be to provide continued support to families as they learn to problem-solve themselves. All levels of the agency will participate in helping the family, but this will be done primarily through the volunteer family. The support that we expect this agency to be able to give will be in areas such as problems with the education system, where, for example, we can help prepare parents to advocate for their children at Identification, Placement, and Review Committee (IPRC) sessions, or with the medical system, where doctors' explanations of treatments and plans need clarification. Behaviour problems are difficult for any family to cope with on a daily basis, and our agency will be available to offer parents support and advice. All levels of the agency will participate in helping the family, but this will be primarily the function of the volunteer family.

Regular questionnaires will be sent out every three months to the families while they are receiving active support to make certain that their needs are being met. After a family no longer needs intensive support, communication will be maintained through phone calls every six months for the first year and a questionnaire after twelve months.

D. COMMUNITY CONTENT

LETTER OF COMMUNITY SUPPORT

Durham Region Children's Aid Society
156 John Street
Oshawa, Ontario
L2F 3G6

April 15, 2011

Mrs. Patricia Caverly
4052 Mason Street
Pickering, Ontario
L2W 5M6

Dear Mrs. Caverly:

It was with interest that I read your preliminary proposal for a funding request for a Post-
Adoptive Family Support Agency.

As you know from our telephone conversations
over the past several years, I have long felt a
need for a well-coordinated family support program following adoption. Ideally, this should be
done by the Children's Aid Society, but we do
not have the staff to provide the long-term support that is so obviously needed in many of the
placements we make.

Please contact this agency as soon as you
receive your funding in order that we may set up
a method of referral.

Your experience in the area of adoption, as well
as your interest in the Durham region, should
prove invaluable in the next few months.

With best wishes,

MCamden

Monica Camden
Adoption Coordinator

E. Program Evaluation

1. Although our long-term goals include the prevention of adoption breakdown, our more immediate goal is to provide support for families. We will therefore judge our effectiveness through feedback from the families that use our service. This will be done partly by monitoring the number of parent-initiated contacts.

2. To this purpose, all telephone and in-person contact will be recorded and discussed at monthly meetings between the coordinator and the area supervisors. Additionally, questionnaires will be sent out to active families every three months to help determine the families' needs and the extent to which we are meeting them. For all families who discharge themselves from our caseload, a follow-up will be done by telephone six months later and by questionnaire twelve months after discharge (see sample questionnaires on pages 80–81).

3. The program will be evaluated by the coordinator in consultation with the area supervisors and the volunteers.

4. The program will be evaluated on an individual family level every three months and on an agency level once a year. A growing caseload and parent-expressed satisfaction through the questionnaires will be the criteria used to judge the overall performance of the program.

FAMILY NEEDS QUESTIONNAIRE

POST-ADOPTION FAMILY SUPPORT AGENCY
1400 BAYLY STREET, UNIT 15A
PICKERING, ONTARIO
L1W 1L4

To help us better meet the needs of your family, we would appreciate it if you would take the time to complete this questionnaire and return it to us.

Family name:

Address:

Phone number:

1. How often do you talk to your worker each month?

2. How long are these contacts usually?

3. Who usually initiates them?

4. Are they helpful?

5. Do you feel better able to cope with your child/family after these contacts?

6. Has your worker helped you contact any other agency?

7. If so, was this helpful?

8. Do you wish to continue this program?

9. Is there any other way we can help you?

FOLLOW-UP QUESTIONNAIRE

POST-ADOPTION FAMILY SUPPORT AGENCY
1400 BAYLY STREET, UNIT 15A
PICKERING, ONTARIO
L1W 1L4

It has now been six months since you expressed the desire not to continue with our program. We are interested to know how your family is doing and whether you feel that our program was useful to your family.

We would appreciate it if you would fill out the following questionnaire and mail it back to us. If we can be of any further service to your family, please contact us.

1. How is your adoptive child doing currently?
   At home?
   At school?
   In the community?

2. Do you feel that your family is reasonably stable at this point?

3. Do you feel at this point that the adoption process has been a positive one for your family?

   If possible, can you explain why or why not?

4. Do you wish any further contact from us?
   By phone?
   By in-person visit?

5. Would you be willing to become a volunteer family? (Training would be provided.)

F. ESTIMATE OF RESOURCES REQUIRED

1. a. The total cost of this program for the fiscal year May 1, 2011, to April 30, 2012, will be $415 550.
   b. The total amount of funds requested from the Ministry of Community Services will be $297 550.

2. The total amount of funds that will be given to this project from community groups in the Durham region is $118 000.

3. Operational Budget
   a. Salaries
Coordinator	@$60 000	$ 60 000
Area supervisors (4)	@$50 000	$ 200 000
Area supervisors, part-time (2)	@$25 000	$ 50 000
Secretary	@$35 000	$ 35 000

   b. Benefits @14% $ 48 300

   c. Staff travel
Coordinator	@$500	$ 500
Area supervisors	@$250	$ 1 500

   d. Staff training @$200 $ 1 400

   e. Supplies
desks (2)	@$150	$ 300
chairs (2)	@$170	$ 340
stacking chairs (8)	@$35	$ 280
stationery	@$1000/year	$ 1 000
file cabinet	@$120	$ 120
fax machine	@$130	$ 130

   f. Computer/e-mail and Web access @$3000 $ 3 000

   g. Food costs @$25/month $ 300

   h. Premises rent @$800/month $ 9 600

   i. Other services
phone	@$40/month	$ 480
long-distance	@$1500/year	$ 1 500

j. Utilities/taxes	N/A	N/A
k. Insurance	N/A	N/A
l. Repairs/ maintenance	@$300/year	$ 300
m. Replacements	N/A	N/A
n. New furnishings/ equipment	@$1000	$ 1 000
o. Vehicle operation/ maintenance	N/A	N/A
p. Advertising/ promotion	@$500/year	$ 500
q. Other	N/A	N/A
Total costs		$415 550.00
Start-up costs		$ 2 170.00
Yearly operating costs		$413 380.00

EXPLORATIONS

6.1 With your partner or in a small group, discuss the strengths and weaknesses of this proposal. Write a memo to your teacher summarizing your group's conclusions.

6.2 You are a staff member of the funding body receiving this proposal. Write a memo to your superior advising that the proposal either receive further consideration for funding or be declined.

6.3 As a staff member of the funding body receiving this proposal, write a letter to the proposal's author refusing her request for funding because the funding body cannot afford to support her program at this time.

6.4 Assume the Post-Adoption Family Support Agency is in operation. Write a letter referring an adoptive family to the agency.

6.5 You are a volunteer with the Post-Adoption Family Support Agency. Write a progress report to your supervisor on one of your client families.

CHAPTER 7

RESEARCHING AND WRITING
A FORMAL REPORT

Overview: This chapter introduces the writing of a formal report. Chapter 8 will provide an example of such a report.

THE DIFFERENCE BETWEEN
A FORMAL REPORT AND
A RESEARCH PAPER

You have doubtless written several research papers during your academic career. Generally, research papers recount information on a given topic to a specific audience—usually, the teacher who assigned it. A research paper is often written to prove a thesis dealing with an academic topic that is at a slight remove from the nitty-gritty of reality. Writing a research paper is both interesting and valuable, but it differs from writing a formal report in some crucial ways.

Formal reports are always grounded in the world we live in. They report on real situations and issues and recommend action in response to data collected and conclusions drawn in particular circumstances. A formal report's audience is the people who could take action on its recommendations. Even if the formal report is written only to raise awareness of an issue and to provide information, the possibility for action is always there. Writers always draw conclusions and makes recommendations—otherwise, it's not a formal report, but a research paper.

STRUCTURE OF A FORMAL REPORT

Formal reports have a conventional structure, which has grown out of the needs of the audience. This structure, known by the acronym SIDCRA, comprises the following sections: summary, introduction, discussion, conclusions and recommendations, and appendix.

SUMMARY

The report opens with a *summary*, which provides a brief overview of the material in the report and a condensed look at its recommendations. The summary provides a snapshot of the report. It orients the principal readers of the report, its audience, as well as acting as an information tool for those who may not be reading the full report, but who do need to learn its major findings and recommendations. The summary is always brief, preferably no more than a page in length. Its purpose is to provide a synopsis, no more. For this reason, the summary is usually written last, despite its primary position. A few highly organized people may be able to write the summary first and live up to it exactly in writing the formal report, but that is generally not the way writing works. The writing of the report itself often will open up possibilities undreamt of at the beginning of the process. So hold off on the summary until the end, to avoid straitjacketing your ideas.

INTRODUCTION

The summary is followed by an *introduction*, which does just what it says—it introduces the reader to the issues that the report deals with. The introduction may detail the reasons for writing the report (Why did someone bother to research and write about these issues?); describe the scope of the report (What will the report consider and what will it leave out? Where will the boundary lines of the issues be drawn?); and provide any background information necessary to understand or evaluate the report (What does the reader need to know beforehand for an informed reading of the report?). Because the introduction is simply the beginning of the report, it is generally quite short.

DISCUSSION

The main body of the report is called the *discussion*. This section presents information and discusses issues in a straightforward, logical way. The discussion section provides the basis for the conclusions and recommendations to be drawn in the report. It is essential that any material presented in this section be accurate and complete. In other words, writers should not ignore data or information that does not conveniently fit the conclusions they wish to draw. If one is to be an ethical writer, a writer with integrity, one cannot ignore data that would refute one's conclusions. Rather, writers must think through the issues honestly and attempt to understand *all* the data available. The aim is not to convince the reader at all costs, but to recommend the right action, or the best action, given the circumstances. Writers must be aware of shades of grey, and be honest with themselves and the reader. Writers must also be prepared to change their minds and even start the report over if the data leads them to different conclusions.

CONCLUSIONS AND RECOMMENDATIONS

The discussion is followed by *conclusions and recommendations*, sometimes united and sometimes presented as separate sections, depending on what works best in the particular writing situation. Conclusions should follow logically from the material presented in the discussion, and recommendations should be based on the conclusions drawn. Writers should not go off on a tangent in these sections, introducing new material or drawing conclusions unconnected with the discussion. Conclusions and recommendations are sometimes presented in list format and are often numbered.

APPENDIX

Finally, some reports will also have an *appendix* (or *appendices*), which presents detailed material referred to in the report or related material that would have broken the flow of the report. Examples of appendices include detailed charts or tables. This textbook, although not a formal report, has two appendices, which provide material that is related to the issues discussed in the text but that is supplemental rather than required. Appendices sometimes serve the function of providing material for some readers who want or need the additional discussion, which not all readers may require.

OTHER TYPES OF FORMAL REPORTS

Other types of formal reports have structures that might be somewhat different from the SIDCRA structure. For instance, you might at some time be called upon to write a cost/benefit analysis or a comparison of several alternatives with a recommendation of the best alternative. However, the SIDCRA structure underlies most reports, with variations to suit the needs of each writing situation. All formal reports share the basic characteristic of presenting material in a logical fashion in order to draw conclusions and make recommendations. If you understand the basic structure of a formal report and its defining features, you can easily branch out into other types of reports.

In Chapter 8 you will find an example of a formal report. It is assumed to be written by a staff member in a youth literacy program. The program, designed to help young unemployed adults acquire generic skills such as reading, writing, and math, has a high percentage of clients who are learning disabled. The staff member heard about a treatment for people with reading problems and decided to learn more about it. After doing some research, the staff member wrote the formal report to recommend that the agency explore the treatment further and have an expert in the treatment visit the agency and screen some of the clients. The staff member chose to write a formal report rather than a memo or e-mail because those making the decision on her recommendation need a fair amount of information in order to make an informed choice. The memo or e-mail format would be inappropriate because the writer's purpose and the needs of the audience could not be met in that smaller structure.

(A note on format: Formal reports are generally written in full block format. See the report in Chapter 8 for an example of the typical look of a formal report.)

SUMMARY

Most reports use the SIDCRA structure:

I. Summary
II. Introduction
III. Discussion
IV. Conclusions
V. Recommendations
VI. Appendix

EXPLORATIONS

7.1 Write a formal report on one of the following topics. Remember that your report must draw conclusions and make recommendations. Some of the topics will require that you determine for yourself the reason for the formal report (i.e., what call to action you might make).

a. You have investigated several possible overseas trips that your agency, which supports disabled travellers, might sponsor. Write a formal report to the agency board with your recommendations for an overseas trip. Be as specific as possible.

b. You have been asked to recommend ways your agency could alleviate or prevent burnout in its workers. Write a formal report to the management board.

c. You have been asked by a local parent group to write a report on setting up home daycare programs. Write the report.

d. Your supervisor has asked you to write a report on future trends in your profession, to be presented to the professional development committee of your organization. Write the report.

e. Your organization is interested in setting up a wilderness trek expedition. Write a formal report to your supervisor, setting out your recommendations for the expedition. Be as specific as possible, perhaps including the recommended client group, expedition structure, and costing of such an expedition.

f. A seniors' lobby group has asked you to write a formal report on support needed for home care of aging parents. Write the report.

g. The parent committee of your agency has asked you to write a report on sexuality in the developmentally delayed teenager. Write the report, keeping in mind that it is not a research paper. It should make recommendations the agency could implement.

h. A number of staff members are retiring, and your agency would like to take this opportunity to increase the diversity of its staff. You have been asked to prepare a report on hiring practices that would allow the agency to meet this objective. Write the report.

i. You have been asked by your supervisor to explore whether introducing First Nations spirituality practices might reduce recidivism in your adolescent clients. Write a report, with recommendations.

j. Your community has a popular amusement park or entertainment venue that has limited accessibility for persons with disabilities. Your agency wishes to advocate for improvements in this area. Write a report recommending changes the park/venue should make. Use a real park or venue as a basis for the report. If you do not actually have one in your area, use the Internet to research an appropriate setting on which to base your report.

k. Your supervisor is concerned about the impact of social networking in the workplace. Write a report with specific recommendations for agency action in this area.

l. You are working as a CYW in a school, and the principal has approached you with concerns about the students' social networking. Write a report that can be shared with staff. Be sure to include specific recommendations.

CHAPTER 8

EXAMPLE OF A FORMAL REPORT

Overview: This chapter presents a formal report that is based on Internet research.

Scotopic Sensitivity Syndrome
and the Irlen Treatment:
A Possible Aid to Learning-Disabled
Clients at Literacy Links

Prepared by:
Twyla Mansooti
Report Distributed: December 10, 2010
Prepared for: Literacy Links

I. SUMMARY

Scotopic sensitivity syndrome (SSS) is a perceptual disorder that may affect many learning-disabled individuals. It was first identified by Helen Irlen. Its symptoms include sensitivity to brightness, difficulty with visual resolution, difficulties both in sustaining focus and in exercising an effective span of focus, and poor depth perception. The disorder is manifested in poor reading skills and in general strain when reading.

Treatment for individuals with scotopic sensitivity syndrome consists of providing coloured lenses that filter out the portion of the spectrum that is causing interference. Treatment does not cure learning disabilities, nor is it effective for all individuals with SSS.

The scientific community has not accepted the existence of SSS or endorsed the Irlen treatment. However, much anecdotal evidence attests to its efficacy.

It is recommended that Literacy Links continue to study the possible benefits of this approach, specifically by

- contacting institutions that use the Irlen treatment.
- conducting a literature review on the treatment.
- arranging a presentation by an Irlen assessor.
- arranging for a Literacy Links staff member to be trained as an Irlen assessor, if deemed appropriate after the investigation of the treatment is completed.

II. INTRODUCTION

Counsellors at Literacy Links have long noted the high incidence among our clients of specific learning disabilities. Many of our clients are of average or above-average intelligence, yet

---

their academic performance has been substandard. Many have dropped out of formal education in despair. At Literacy Links we attempt to undo the years of frustration by applying teaching methods and technologies that will provide our clients with strategies to cope with their disabilities. For instance, we teach dysgraphic clients morphological spelling to provide an alternative to phonological spelling. We also introduce our clients to various adaptive technologies such as reading machines, voice-activated software, and spell checkers. As counsellors, we continue to develop professionally in order to best serve our clients.

One area of that professional development is the seeking out of alternative pedagogies, treatments, and technologies that might be of benefit to our clients. An approach that holds promise for persons with learning disabilities is the identification and treatment of scotopic sensitivity syndrome.

III. DISCUSSION

Scotopic sensitivity syndrome was first identified by Helen Irlen, who at the time was an educational psychologist working with clients at the Adult Disabilities Clinic at California State University, Long Beach. Many of Irlen's clients reported difficulties with reading that were similar. These difficulties appeared to be centred in the area of visual perception.

Characteristics and Symptoms of Scotopic Sensitivity Syndrome

Some of these difficulties with reading, which not all clients experienced, include

- sensitivity to fluorescent lighting, which led clients to read in dim light
- reading slowly, hesitantly, and inaccurately, with poor comprehension

- skipping or misreading words
- reading word by word, rather than in larger units
- having difficulty with tracking
- experiencing eyestrain, often accompanied by headache or nausea
- having difficulty copying written material (Whiting, 1993)

Irlen isolated several symptoms of SSS:

- light sensitivity, i.e., sensitivity to glare, brightness, and intensity of lighting conditions
- inadequate background accommodation, i.e., difficulty in accommodating contrast between figure and ground in printed material
- difficulty with print resolution, i.e., experiencing perceptual distortions such as print that moves, shifts, or disappears completely
- restricted span of recognition, i.e., difficulties in dealing with a span of text as opposed to small, discrete items (letters, syllables, words)
- difficulty with sustained attention, i.e., inability to stay on task
- poor depth perception, sometimes manifested in clumsiness or poor sports performance

Treatment of Scotopic Sensitivity Syndrome

To aid her clients who appeared to have SSS, Irlen developed a treatment using visual filters. She began by simply applying coloured overlays over the printed page, but found that not all SSS sufferers benefited from the overlays alone. She then developed coloured glasses to screen out the portion of the spectrum that caused the problem in SSS sufferers. The required tint varies from client to client. Approximately 150 or more tints are used, and the glasses must be prescribed by a trained assessor.

Reaction to the Irlen Approach

Reaction to Irlen's treatment has been mixed. In 1992 the American Academy of Pediatrics and Ophthalmology released a statement that concluded that treatments such as tinted lenses have not been helpful in the treatment of dyslexia and related disorders. The scientific community as a whole has failed to endorse Irlen's treatment and, indeed, to concede that SSS even exists, stating that evidence of SSS is anecdotal and biased, and improvements in reading comfort result from the placebo effect.

However, there appears to be a growing body of popular support, similar to the support given to complementary therapies that are also denigrated by the scientific community. As well, Whiting, Robinson, and Parrott present a summary of research on the treatment and a six-year follow-up report, which concludes that there are "benefits of various kinds over a long time span, noticeably in improved visual perceptions of print, and greater ease of reading" (Whiting, Robinson, and Parrott, n.d.).

Limitations of the Irlen Approach

Tinted filters do not cure learning disabilities. Indeed, the two difficulties are separate. Learning-disabled individuals who benefit from tinted lenses still require direct teaching of reading skills. The lenses may remove a barrier to learning, but they cannot produce learning on their own.

As well, not all individuals with reading difficulties have SSS. The treatment is actually a three-stage process: first, a complete eye exam is conducted to rule out other vision problems; second, a prescreening is done to determine whether the client has SSS; and third, the appropriate tint is matched to the client.

Not all individuals with SSS can be helped by tinted glasses. A percentage of clients with SSS fail to find a lens that improves visual processing.

Costs of the Irlen Treatment

The Irlen treatment is costly. Only trained Irlen assessors can screen clients, and the process is lengthy. An ophthalmologist examines each client. If the examination indicates no other visual problems that might account for the client's difficulties, an Irlen assessor screens the client to determine the presence of SSS. Following a positive SSS screening, the assessor conducts the lengthy process of determining the lens that provides maximum benefit for the client.

IV. CONCLUSIONS

1. At this time, the scientific community does not accept the Irlen approach, as there is little scientific validation of its claimed benefits. However, several effective complementary therapies are also not accepted by the scientific community. Legitimate breakthroughs are often as likely to face initial rejection as are quackeries. Therefore, lack of acceptance by the scientific community is not reason enough to reject this treatment.
2. Much anecdotal evidence supports the efficacy of the treatment for some learning-disabled individuals. Some of these apparent successes may be due to the placebo effect, but the volume of support indicates that this approach merits further consideration.
3. The approach does not claim to cure learning disabilities, nor does it claim to help all SSS sufferers.
4. Irlen screening is costly. However, the potential benefits to individuals with reading problems are immeasurable.

V. RECOMMENDATIONS

1. Other institutions are using the Irlen treatment with their clients. I recommend that we contact staff at those institutions to discuss their experience with this treatment.

2. I recommend that time be allotted to a staff member to conduct an extensive literature review of this treatment.
3. I recommend that we invite a trained Irlen assessor into our agency to make a presentation on the method.
4. Should the approach appear to hold promise for our clients, I recommend that a staff member be trained as an Irlen assessor.

VI. APPENDIX

References

Whiting, P. R. (1993). *How difficult can reading be?* Retrieved Nov. 27, 2010, from http://www.dyslexiaservices.com.au/ Reading_Difficulty.htm

Whiting, P. R., Robinson, G. L. W., & Parrott, C. F. (n.d.). *Irlen coloured filters for reading: A six-year follow-up.* Retrieved Nov. 27, 2010, from http://www.dyslexiaservices. com.au/Six-Year_Follow-Up.htm

Note: The research I conducted for this brief report was primarily Internet-based. In addition to the website cited above, please see the following sites:

http://www.irlen.com
http://www.irlen.org.uk (contains an extensive bibliography)
http://www.ldrc.ca/contents/view_article/207
http://www.ldrc.ca/contents/view_article.php?id=210

Whiting, Robinson, and Parrott offer access to valuable print sources in this area in the notes to their article cited above. Also, see the book Helen Irlen has published on her treatment:

Irlen, H. (2005). *Reading by the colors: Overcoming dyslexia and other reading disabilities through the Irlen method* (Revised ed.). New York: Berkley Publishing Group.

EXPLORATIONS

8.1 With a partner or in a small group, discuss the strengths and weaknesses of this formal report. Write a memo to your teacher summarizing your conclusions.

8.2 You are the recipient of this formal report. Write a memo to your manager advising that it either receive further consideration or be declined.

8.3 Literacy Links has implemented the recommendations of this report. You are a worker with another agency and have heard about the new program. You have a client you feel would benefit from the screening. Write a letter of referral for this client.

8.4 The screening program has been in place for six months. Write a progress report to your supervisor about the program.

CHAPTER 9

RESEARCH SKILLS: GATHERING DATA USING PRIMARY AND SECONDARY SOURCES

Overview: This chapter discusses gathering the data for any writing task using either primary or secondary sources. Using primary sources, you gather the data directly yourself; using secondary sources, you use data someone else has gathered. Primary sources include interviews, observations, and surveys. Secondary sources include library resources, the Internet, and literature reviews.

GATHERING THE DATA: PRIMARY RESEARCH

In order to write, you must have something to say. Sometimes your own experiences and prior knowledge provide enough content for a piece of writing. At other times, you'll find that you must do some research. There are two basic types of research: primary and secondary. We'll look at primary research first.

Primary research involves going out and finding data yourself, rather than depending solely on library or Internet research or on data that someone else has gathered. Both types of research have a place in the writing process.

How do we find information without using books or the Internet? We can talk and listen to other people (interviewing), we can watch other people (observing), and we can ask several people relevant questions and then analyze their responses (surveying). Entire courses could be organized around each of these techniques; this chapter will provide a brief introduction to each.

INTERVIEWS

Suppose you're interested in the mainstreaming of children with disabilities (i.e., placing children with physical or mental challenges in "regular" classrooms). You've read articles about mainstreaming, but you want to get closer to the issue. What can you do?

You might decide to interview the mother of a main-streamed child, the child's teacher, other students, or the child with disabilities. How would you go about doing this?

The hardest part might be finding someone to interview. You could ask your teachers for a lead, call the schools in your area, or call the relevant society or support group. You could ask around, mentioning your need to friends, neighbours, and people you work with. You would probably be surprised at how many people you know who could introduce you to someone you might interview (I know at least four different families who could be interviewed on this subject).

Once you've found an interview subject, what do you do? How do you conduct a successful interview? *Be prepared.* The person granting the interview is doing you a favour. You owe that person an effective use of his or her time. Plan your questions carefully in advance. Know what you want to ask, and why. Know as much as possible about the topic before you do the interview.

Although you should be well prepared, you shouldn't dominate the interview. Control it subtly. Put your subject at ease. Listen to him or her, and let your questions grow logically from the discussion. I once was subjected to a very strange job interview. I was interviewed by a team of three people. They were interviewing several people for a teaching position and wanted to be fair to every candidate. They had therefore decided to ask every candidate the same questions in the same order. It was clear to me, as interviewee, that this plan was not working. One of them would ask a question, I would answer, and another would be interested in my response and would begin to follow it up, only to be reined in by the person whose turn it was to ask the next question. Too rigid an interview format gets you nowhere. Often, travelling down the little side paths leads us to make our greatest discoveries.

So go with the flow, but maintain some control. Don't waste the interview time; steer the conversation in the right direction. But always listen carefully for the little clue to be followed up.

Remember the use of silence. If your subject doesn't immediately respond to a question, don't jump in with another question. Maybe your subject is thinking! Don't be anxious to fill the silence. Your subject will eventually start talking again—to fill up the silence! (And keep in mind cultural differences. In some cultures it is disrespectful to answer without taking proper time for reflection.)

Just a few other comments on interviewing: In arranging the interview, be courteous to the person you are interviewing by asking what date and time would be best. Explain what you are doing and why. Ask if your interviewee would like a list of possible questions beforehand, in order to be prepared. If you wish to tape the interview, *ask permission*. It is illegal to tape someone without permission.

The day before the time set for the interview, call to confirm that the subject is still able to see you. Arrive on time for the interview. At the end of the interview, thank your subject. Sending a written thank-you a few days later is also a thoughtful touch.

While you're interviewing, pay attention to body language. People do not always tell the truth during interviews or while responding to surveys. Use your judgment in deciding what to believe. And watch your own body language. Display an impartial attitude, showing interest but repressing expressions such as shock, surprise, and disbelief.

What if you're not able to meet with the interviewee in person? Although it is sometimes more difficult, you can also conduct interviews by telephone, e-mail, or texting.

Many of the considerations noted for in-person interviews are also true for these kinds of interviews. However, in these cases you are hampered by being unable to see the interviewee. I have been interviewed by telephone, and I have found it somewhat frustrating. I became aware of how much I relied on nonverbal signals when communicating. I could not gauge the effect my words were having on the interviewer, except through his verbal feedback. Consequently, I depended more on his verbal responsiveness instead of on nonverbal feedback such as head nodding and other body language, which help face-to-face interviews move along more smoothly. I had a sense of speaking into a vacuum. A telephone interviewer, then, must be careful to offer appropriate verbal feedback to make up for the lack of nonverbal feedback, without, of course, short-circuiting the interviewee's train of thought.

An electronic interview, interestingly, doesn't seem to offer the same frustrations as the telephone interview, perhaps because our expectations are different. An interview held in real time via texting can be quite intriguing and rewarding. In fact, that slight time delay necessitated by typing in one's questions or responses allows for a degree of thoughtfulness that is sometimes missing in face-to-face interaction.

OBSERVATIONS

You've done an interview. Now you would like to do an observation. You arrange with the child's teacher to observe her class for an afternoon to see how the other children react to having a disabled child in the classroom. How do you prepare beforehand?

Before doing an observation, it helps to draw up a checklist form. What behaviours are you likely to see? List them on one side of a sheet of paper. Leave space at the bottom to add any other behaviours you might think of later. When you visit the classroom, check off each behaviour as it occurs.

You could also make notes on the progress of the afternoon. What happened? What were the interactions?

One difficulty with observations is that behaviour changes when an observer is present. The children cannot act as though you are not there. Nor can the teacher. Your being there makes a difference. Unless you observe behind a two-way mirror (which is possible in some settings), your presence will alter the data somewhat. However, you can still learn valuable information using observations. Just be aware that your presence did have an impact.

SURVEYS

The last type of primary research we'll look at is the survey. Professional surveys are complicated to design, but informal surveys can yield useful data. The most difficult part of an amateur survey is getting the surveys completed. People often don't want to be bothered. It is essential that the survey be brief, simple, and easy to answer...or no one will fill it out.

Before you develop a survey, you must decide what you want to find out. Let's say you're still working on the main-streaming topic. You want to discover parents' attitudes toward having a developmentally delayed child in the regular class-room. Your questions should focus on discovering their attitudes. However, it might be less than useful to ask straight out what they think of having such children mainstreamed. People want to look their best and, thus, sometimes lie on surveys, whether consciously or unconsciously. Therefore, you need to get at the real truth in a roundabout way.

The survey should be easy to complete. Ask only one thing at a time. Give complete instructions. Explain what the survey is for, and why you are conducting it. Ask concrete questions. Begin with the simplest questions, then move on to more difficult questions.

There are several types of survey questions. The following are some common types of questions (we'll assume you're writing a report on your school's cafeteria):

- *Open-ended:* "What changes would you like to see in cafeteria selections?"

Any answer is possible. The advantage of this type of question is that it will turn up unexpected information. The disadvantage is that the answers are difficult to tabulate.

- *Either-or:* "The cafeteria offers good value for the price charged."

   _____ Yes

   _____ No.

This type of question is easy to tabulate, but its disadvantage is that you give no middle ground. Introducing "Maybe" or "It depends" (on what?) gives a bit more choice, but perhaps not enough.

- *Multiple-choice:* "What is the most important factor in determining whether you will eat in the cafeteria?" (choose only one)

   a. variety
   b. price
   c. taste
   d. my friends eat there
   e. vegetarian food offered
   f. low fat/low calorie choices available
   g. name brand (chain) food available
   h. convenience
   i. weather
   j. comfortable seating
   k. service

The main advantage of this type of question is, again, ease of tabulation; the main disadvantage is that it is almost impossible to cover all possible answers.

- *Scale:* "Please place an X on the scale to indicate how satisfied you are with the cafeteria's food offerings."

Very dissatisfied	Mildly dissatisfied	Somewhat satisfied	Satisfied	Very satisfied

The advantage of this type of question is that it is simple to answer; the disadvantage is that the choices may fail to reflect the diversity and complexity of possible answers.

- *Checklist:* "Which types of food would you like to see offered at lunchtime?" (check as many as apply)

_____ sandwiches
_____ wraps
_____ pizza
_____ burgers
_____ vegetarian
_____ halal
_____ organic
_____ entrées (meat, vegetable, potato)
_____ other (please specify)

A checklist is easy to fill in and tabulate, but length restrictions make it hard to be exhaustive. However, providing space for respondents to add comments can help.

- *Ranking:* "Please rank the following factors by importance in determining whether you will eat in the cafeteria." (1 is the most important):

a. variety
b. price
c. taste
d. my friends eat there
e. vegetarian food offered
f. low fat/low calorie choices available
g. name brand (chain) food available
h. convenience
i. weather
j. comfortable seating
k. service

This type of survey is easy to fill in and tabulate, but, again, it is not exhaustive.

- *Fill in the blank:* "What menu items should the cafeteria add?" _____

This form offers scope for a wide range of answers, but it is difficult to tabulate.

If the survey continues on the back of the sheet, remind the respondent to turn it over ("Continued overleaf" or "Over, please"). This may sound silly, but I have had students ignore the second page of exams, much less surveys!

Always provide space at the bottom of a survey for the respondent's comments. And be sure to say thank-you!

(Once again, note that this has been a brief introduction to primary research, to give you a few tools to gather information. Your teacher may choose to go into more depth at this point, discussing types of survey samples, standard deviation, and so on, but such topics are beyond the range of this text.)

GATHERING THE DATA: SECONDARY RESEARCH

LITERATURE REVIEWS

Secondary research involves going to the library or the library website. Your aim is to do a literature review to find out what people have written about your topic.

Libraries you have dealt with in the past probably used the Dewey Decimal classification (DDC) system. Public libraries usually use Dewey, whereas college and university libraries use the Library of Congress classification (LCC) system. It's not necessary to know the intricacies of the two systems. In each system, areas of knowledge are divided and subdivided: Dewey decimal uses numbers and Library of Congress uses letters and numbers to categorize books. Use the computer to discover the section of the library in which the books you want are located.

But how do you know which books you want? There are a few methods to use in locating books. My favourite, although it is not the quickest, is to find the location of a subject area I'm interested in, then look through the shelves in that area, pull off the interesting-looking books, sit on the floor, and roam about those books for a while. I find that subject area by looking in the *Subject Guide to the Library of Congress Listings*, available at any college or university library. The subject guide will give me the LCC-approved designation for any area of knowledge (the subject under which it is catalogued). I then use the computer to look under that heading, note the call number of books with that subject heading, point myself in the right direction, and settle down for an interesting read.

There are some obvious disadvantages to this method—it is a bit hit-and-miss, after all. But don't rule it out. Browsing through books on an area you're interested in can be productive, as well as pleasant.

If you're in more of a hurry, however, you can search the bibliographies. *Bibliographies* are collections of sources. Someone else has already located relevant books and articles and categorized them for you. Some relevant bibliographies in community service work are

- *Sources of Information in the Social Sciences*
- *Social Sciences Index*
- *Psychological Abstracts*
- *Sociological Abstracts*
- ERIC (Educational Resources Information Center)
- CIJE (*Current Index to Journals in Education*)

Another excellent source is a CD-ROM or online database. If you do not already know how to use databases, ask your college librarian for a training session. Most college libraries have a tutorial on their website.

You may have access to the collections of more than one library in your community. Other college and university libraries may offer interlibrary loans. There may be specialized libraries available, run by community service agencies or government departments. Spread your net wide in finding secondary sources.

THE INTERNET

Net surfers sometimes read material on the Internet uncritically. By this I mean that they accord material found on the Net the same status as print material (i.e., articles in books or in professional journals). You should never approach any material uncritically, but there is one crucial difference between

Research Skills

the Internet and other print sources. *Anyone with access to a computer and certain software can publish on the Net.* Much trash may be published in books or in journals, but that material has undergone a screening process by editors, reviewers, a panel of experts in the field, and so on. But *no one* scrutinizes material on the Internet before it is published. If I wished, and if I had the appropriate technology, I could publish on my website a definitive guide to chaos theory as it relates to the reproductive capacity of Australian marsupials, even though I know nothing whatsoever about that topic or, indeed, if it is a valid topic at all. If you accessed my website as part of a search on a project on kangaroos, how would you know that I was not an expert?

Believing in the expertise of a pseudo-expert on marsupials is regrettable but probably not the end of the world. However, in the field with which you are involved, the field of human services, believing quacks can be dangerous. Treat whatever you find on the Web with appropriate caution. Ask yourself some basic questions:

- Who is this "expert"?
- What are his or her claims to expertise? Are they valid?
- What claims is this person making?
- What is his or her evidence?
- Is that evidence valid?
- Are there logical flaws in the argument?
- Does this person have a bias or an ideological agenda?
- Can I find independent confirmation for the claims presented?

When you use the Internet with these cautions in mind, it can be a valuable tool that puts the world within your grasp. Use it wisely.

DOCUMENTING YOUR RESEARCH

Why do we document our sources when we write? There are several reasons. First, neglecting to acknowledge where we have obtained material is considered intellectual dishonesty,

---

akin to stealing someone's property. And, indeed, ideas are intellectual property. In a way, stealing a person's ideas is a greater violation than stealing a wallet. In fact, plagiarizing someone's material is a legal offence.

Ethics are not the only reason for documenting sources, however. We also document our sources to help our reader either to look at a topic in greater depth by reading some of our sources or to judge what we have written by considering and evaluating our sources. What do I mean by this?

Our reader may be interested in what we have written and want to find out more about our topic. What better way than to read some of the material we used during our research? It is not uncommon, for instance, for graduate students to track down the sources mentioned in an essay's notes to broaden their understanding of an area. On the other hand, our notes can help a reader to judge the validity of our argument. Were our sources up-to-date? Were they respected in the field? Was our research extensive? Did we miss anything of vital importance?

The conventions of documentation are based on these two complementary purposes: to help our readers both find and evaluate our sources. With that in mind, let's consider what a reader would need to know about a particular source:

- who wrote it (to judge the credibility of the source)
- when it was written (to judge its currency)
- the exact title
- its publishing details

Let's take a look at some sample bibliography entries to see how they include material that will meet the reader's needs. Different fields use different styles of documentation in order to suit their audiences' particular needs. Your field uses the American Psychological Association (APA) style, used in the social sciences.

Many guides to documentation are available, and writers often keep a guide beside them as they work. Few people can keep all the details of a documentation style in their minds. Documentation conventions are like the periodic table— something to be consulted rather than memorized by all but the hardy few. If you don't have one already, download one of the guides listed in Exploration 9.1. Here are some examples of common types of APA reference entries:

Book, one author:

Ashworth, A. (2005). *Sentencing and criminal justice* (4th ed.). Cambridge: Cambridge University Press.

Book, more than one author:

Roberts, J. V., & Hough, M. (2005). *Understanding public attitudes to criminal justice*. Maidenhead: Open University Press.

Article in a collection:

La Prairie, C. (2007). Aboriginal overrepresentation: No single problem, no simple solution. In J. V. Roberts and M. G. Grossman (Eds.), *Criminal justice in Canada: A reader*. Toronto: Nelson.

Article in a journal with continuous pagination:

Leighton, B. (1991). Visions of community policing: Rhetoric and reality in Canada. *Canadian Journal of Criminology, 33,* 485–522.

Article in journal, paginated by issue:

Leighton, B. (2006). Re-visions of community policing: Reality redefined for Canada. *Canadian Law Enforcement Quarterly, 27*(3), 12–23.

Material from Internet:

Valentino, L. (2011). *APA documentation*. Retrieved May 8, 2011, from www.humber.ca/valentin/apadoc.html

EXPLORATIONS

9.1 Useful guides to documentation can be found at the following links:

http://www.macewan.ca/web/services/ims/client/upload/APAjan10.pdf
http://owl.english.purdue.edu/owl/resource/560/01/
http://writing.wisc.edu/Handbook/DocAPA.html
http://www.lib.sfu.ca/help/writing/apa

9.2 For this exploration, you will create a research portfolio. Artists' portfolios contain samples of their work to illustrate their skills. A research portfolio contains items that demonstrate your mastery of research skills. Your instructor will tell you exactly what to include in your portfolio, but it might contain

    a. an interview, both transcript and summary
    b. an observation of a client
    c. a survey
    d. a summary of an article
    e. an evaluation of an article
    f. a literature review on a given topic
    g. an annotated bibliography evaluating three Internet resources on a given topic

9.3 One source of information not mentioned in this chapter is the focus group or small group meeting. Identify an issue on your campus, such as financial aid, daycare for students' children, or accessibility of facilities for students with disabilities. Assemble a small group of students affected by the issue. Get their ideas on the issue. Summarize what they have to say. Write a recommendation to the appropriate person at your school, requesting that some or all of the focus group's suggestions be implemented. (This would also be an appropriate topic for the term-long writing assignment.)

9.4 Choose a public area, either at your school or in your community, where you can observe what is going on around you without arousing suspicion or being intrusive (e.g., if you choose your local bank as an observation spot, you may run into trouble). Determine beforehand what type(s) of behaviour you will be looking for and prepare a checklist, then observe carefully for a predetermined length of time. Summarize your observations in the format your teacher suggests.

9.5 Interview a professional in your field to determine which changes he or she would like to see in the way students in that field are educated. Present your findings to your teacher in the format he or she suggests.

9.6   Make a list of journals of interest to someone in your field that are carried by your school library or available electronically.

9.7   Make a list of bibliographies or databases of use to someone in your field.

9.8   Locate one source from each bibliography or database discovered in Exploration 9.7.

9.9   Visit a website of your choice. Evaluate what you find there, using the questions listed in the chapter as a guide. Report your findings in the format requested by your teacher.

9.10   Write a bibliography entry for each of the following:

- a book with one author
- a book with two authors
- a journal article
- a movie on DVD
- an article in a collection
- a government website

CHAPTER 10

USING GRAPHICS IN REPORTS: BASIC TYPES OF GRAPHICS AND WHEN TO USE THEM

Overview: In reports and presentations, we often use graphics to illustrate a point succinctly. This chapter discusses when and how to use graphics, describes different types of graphics, and provides examples.

WHAT ARE GRAPHICS?

A graphic is any illustration in a report or presentation. You probably are familiar with several types of graphics, such as tables, bar charts, pie charts, line charts or graphs, photos, and cartoons. We will be discussing only the mathematical types of graphics.

WHY USE GRAPHICS?

Graphics are used to communicate information efficiently. Graphics can provide either a quick visual impression to make a point rapidly, or detailed information in an easy-to-understand format.

WHEN DO I USE GRAPHICS?

To repeat, graphics are used to communicate information efficiently. They are used for a purpose. If you have a fancy graphics program on your computer, you may be tempted to overuse graphics. But graphics should be used only if they are relevant to your report or presentation. They must *add* to your communication, not distract the audience's attention from your main point. So as you write, or as you prepare a presentation, ask yourself if a graphic will be the most effective way of conveying your message. If the graphic would merely be a frill, leave it out.

HOW DO I USE GRAPHICS?

Once you have decided to use a graphic, you are faced with two decisions: which type to use and where to place the graphic. You also need to consider graphics conventions—that is, how to present your graphics in a format that is standard in the business and professional community.

GRAPHICS CONVENTIONS

Every graphic must have the following:

1. a number. As we'll discuss below, tables are numbered separately from all other graphics. The number makes it easy to refer to the proper graphic in the text of your report or presentation.
2. an explanatory title, so the audience knows what the graphic is supposed to show and is prepared to understand it.
3. labels on columns and rows, so the audience can decipher the graphic.
4. a unit of measurement, such as dollars, thousands of dollars, hundreds of people, millions of housing units, and so on.
5. any explanatory notes that are necessary to understand the graphic; especially important are definitions of key terms.
6. the source of the graphic, if you did not gather the numbers yourself.

Take a look at the sample graphic (Table 10.1) below.

Table 10.1

NUMBER OF VIOLENT CRIMES BY SEX OF VICTIM AND RELATIONSHIP TO ACCUSED, REPORTED TO A SUBSET OF POLICE SERVICES, 2007

Relationship of accused to victim	Total		Sex of victim			
			Female		Male	
	number	%	number	%	number	%
Total victims of violent crime	**335,676**	**100**	**167,994**	**100**	**167,682**	**100**
Total family	75,779	23	54,186	32	21,593	13
Total spouse	40,165	12	33,227	20	6,938	4
Current spouse[1]	28,637	9	23,726	14	4,911	3
Ex-spouse[2]	11,528	3	9,501	6	2,027	1
Total other family	35,614	11	20,959	12	14,655	9
Parent	11,064	3	6,412	4	4,652	3
Child	6,640	2	4,282	3	2,358	1
Sibling	8,317	2	4,782	3	3,535	2
Extended family	9,593	3	5,483	3	4,110	2
Total friends/ acquaintances	125,918	38	66,412	40	59,506	35
Boyfriend/girlfriend	19,851	6	16,333	10	3,518	2
Ex-boyfriend/ girlfriend	11,886	4	9,817	6	2,069	1
Close friend	11,143	3	5,534	3	5,609	3
Casual acquaintance	64,858	19	27,754	17	37,104	22
Business relationship	12,534	4	4,767	3	7,767	5
Criminal relationship	1,863	1	399	0	1,464	1
Authority figure	3,783	1	1,808	1	1,975	1
Stranger	77,250	23	22,888	14	54,362	32
Unknown	56,729	17	24,508	15	32,221	19

[1] Includes legally married and common-law partners.

[2] Includes separated and divorced partners.

Note. Percentages may not total 100 percent due to rounding. Excludes incidents where the sex and/or age of the victim was unknown. Current spouse and ex-spouse categories include victims aged 15 to 98.

Source: Statistics Canada, Study: Family Violence and Shelters for Abused Women 2007, *The Daily*, 11-001-XIE, Thursday, October 15, 2009; http://www.statcan.gc.ca/daily-quotidien/091015/dq091015b-eng.htm

Note the *number*, Table 10.1, which indicates that it is the first table in Chapter 10. Note the *title*, which indicates exactly what the subject of this table is: the number of violent crimes reported to police in 2007, broken down by sex of victim and relationship to the accused perpetrator. We know exactly what to expect because of the explanatory title. The *unit of measurement* (number) is also given in the table. We know that this is the exact number of violent crimes (rather than, for example, needing to multiply by 100 if the unit of measurement were given in hundreds). Percentages are also given. Note the clear use of *labels* on columns and rows. *Notes* are provided to explain portions of the table that might otherwise be open to misinterpretation (for example, whether common-law partners are included in the category "spouse"). Finally, the *source* indicates exactly where this graphic came from.

TYPES OF GRAPHICS

Of the many types of graphics, I will discuss the following major types: tables, line charts, bar charts, and pie charts. There is a "right" graphic for every communication job. Which you choose depends on your purpose and on your data.

Tables

Tables, as I have mentioned, are in a class by themselves. They are numbered as tables, whereas all other graphics are numbered as figures or charts (whether you number all the others as figures or number them all as charts is up to you, but choose one and be consistent).

Tables present detailed information in an accessible format. They do not make a quick visual impression, but they do allow the reader to extract particular pieces of information. For example, look back at Table 10.1. In 2007, how many females were victimized by a boyfriend? By an ex-boyfriend? How many by a casual acquaintance?

Those answers are relatively easy to find. Now let me ask another question, and see how quickly you can answer. Which are the four categories of victimization in which male victims outnumbered female victims? Can you tell me in 30 seconds? Why not?

You could have answered that last question immediately if you were looking at another type of graphic, such as a bar chart. Tables are great for providing detailed information. Their limitation is that they require some work on the part of the reader. Readers must think for themselves by comparing data and making inferences. The advantage, of course, is that the data are there, rich and available for exploration. The drawback is that sometimes, as a writer, you may want to do the readers' thinking for them.

One last note about tables. There are two styles: open and closed gridlines. (See Table 10.2 for an example of an open table.) Open tables are much preferred today, perhaps because they are more attractive and considerably less intimidating than closed tables. Complicated tables such as Table 10.1 need to be closed. Consider if the entirety of data is needed to make your point. If it is, keep it all and keep it closed. If you only really need a subset of the data, however, keep it simple, and keep it open!

Line Charts

Chances are you learned to do a line chart back in high-school math class. You had an *x* and a *y* axis (or ordinate and abscissa, if you want to get fancy) and you were given some values and told to plot the chart. Line charts are appropriate for showing the rise or fall of what is graphed. Look at the line chart in Figure 10.1.

Did the number of one-person households go up or down between 1956 and 1971? During which 15-year period did the five-or-more-person household remain relatively stable before dropping precipitously? What is the trend in one-person households in Canada?

All of these questions are easy to answer by looking at the line chart. If I were to ask you to give me numbers exact to the last digit, however, you would have more difficulty answering. Line charts provide approximations.

Table 10.2

LIVING ARRANGEMENTS OF SENIORS AGED 65 AND OVER BY SEX AND AGE GROUP, CANADA, 2001

Sex	Age group	Living alone	Living with spouse or partner (no children)	Living with children	Living in health care institution	Other living arrangements[1]	Total
			%				(numbers)
Males	Total 65+	16.0	61.4	13.3	4.9	4.4	1,666,400
	65–74	14.0	64.4	15.4	2.1	4.0	1,008,735
	75–84	18.3	60.7	10.2	6.2	4.6	533,705
	85+	22.7	39.5	8.5	22.6	6.7	123,960
Females	Total 65+	34.8	35.4	12.1	9.2	8.4	2,224,395
	65–74	28.2	48.1	14.1	2.3	7.3	1,135,475
	75–84	42.8	27.7	10.8	9.6	9.2	798,300
	85+	38.5	7.2	8.4	35.4	10.6	290,620

[1] Includes living with other relatives, e.g., a niece or nephew, or with non-relatives, e.g., a lodger.

Source: Adapted from Statistics Canada, Profile of Canadian Families and Households: Diversification Continues, *2001 Census*, 96F0030XIE2001003, October 2002; http://www.statcan.gc.ca/bsolc/olc-cel/olc-cel?lang=eng&catno=96F0030X2001003

Figure 10.1

PERCENTAGE OF ONE-PERSON AND FIVE-OR-MORE-PERSON
HOUSEHOLDS IN CANADA, 1941–2006

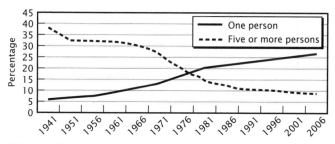

Note. Comparable historical data are not available for census years prior to 1941.

Source: Statistics Canada, Housing and Shelter Costs, *2006 Census,* 97-554-XIE2006001,
July 2008; http://www.statcan.gc.ca/bsolc/olc-cel/olc-cel?lang=eng&catno=97-554-X2006001

Look back at Tables 10.1 and 10.2. What sorts of details could you provide from these tables that you could not provide from a line chart? What advantage, though, does a line chart have over a table?

A few things to note about line charts. Keep the number of lines to a minimum. Generally, three or four lines make for readability in a line chart; any more, especially if they intersect, and the chart looks like a nest of snakes—and who wants to get involved with a nest of snakes? The other important thing to note about line charts is the way one line is differentiated from another. *Differentiate by weight, not by colour.* By this I mean draw one line as a series of dots, one as dashes, and so on, or vary the thickness or density of grey, rather than making one line blue, one green, and so on. With the popularity of colour photocopiers, this piece of advice will soon be dated, but currently, reports are generally copied on a standard black-and-white photocopier. And what happens to all those lovely blue and green lines? They all come out black. Therefore, until the day comes when everyone has a colour photocopier, differentiate by weight, not by colour. Figure 10.2 is another example of a line chart.

Figure 10.2

PERSONS IN COMMON-LAW COUPLES

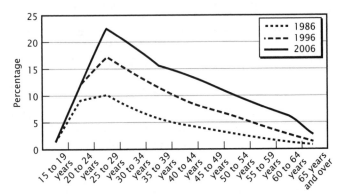

Source: Statistics Canada, Families and Households, *2006 Census,* 97-553-XWE2006001, September 2007; http://www.statcan.gc.ca/bsolc/olc-cel/olc-cel?catno=97-553-XWE2006001&lang=eng

Bar Charts

Look at the bar chart in Figure 10.3.

Which was the most common family type in 1986? In 2006? By 2006, which family type had experienced the greatest rate of change?

Chances are you could answer the first two questions easily, but the third may have given you some difficulty. Bar charts give a quick visual impression, but they are vague on the small details. Sometimes a value will be added at the top of each bar, as in this example, so that exact figures can be given. Whether you do this depends on your needs. Figure 10.3 is a vertical bar chart. Figure 10.4 is an example of a horizontal bar chart.

Pie Charts

Pie charts are another type of graphic with which you are probably familiar. They make a quick visual impression. Consider Figure 10.5.

Which was the most common decision in adult criminal court in 2003?

Figure 10.3

CANADIAN FAMILY STRUCTURE, 1986, 1996, 2006

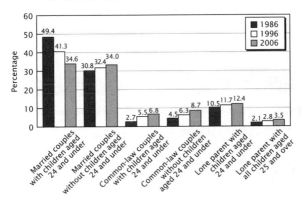

Note. Historical comparisons for census families, particularly lone-parent families, must be interpreted with caution due to conceptual changes in 2001.

Source: Statistics Canada, Families and Households, *2006 Census,* 97-553-XWE2006001, September 2007; http://www.statcan.gc.ca/bsolc/olc-cel/olc-cel?catno=97-553-XWE2006001&lang=eng

Figure 10.4

POPULATION WITH DISABILITIES, BY PROVINCE, 2001

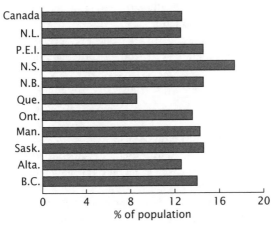

Source: Adapted from Statistics Canada, *A Profile of Disability in Canada,* 2001, 89-577, December 2003.

Figure 10.5

CRIMINAL CODE CASES IN ADULT CRIMINAL COURT,
BY TYPE OF DECISION, 2003

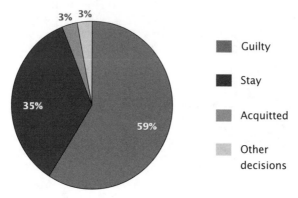

Source: Adapted from the Statistics Canada *CANSIM database* http://cansim2.statcan.gc.ca,
table 252-0015, date of extraction.

When creating pie charts, keep the following guidelines
in mind:

1. Make the slices of your pie visually accurate. If you are
   drawing the graphic manually rather than on a computer,
   use a compass and protractor.
2. Don't make the slices too tiny. If you have several small
   categories, group them together under "other" or "miscel-
   laneous."
3. Be sure your values add up to your basic whole unit, such
   as 100 percent or $1.

Surface Charts/Stacked Bar Charts

A less common graphic type that is useful in some situations is
known as a surface chart or stacked bar chart. It is similar in con-
cept to a pie chart, adding up to 100 percent or a whole unit, but
it is better able to show comparisons. Look at Figure 10.6. Not
only can you get a sense from the graphic of the composition of

Figure 10.6

MARITAL STATUS OF CANADIAN POPULATION 15 YEARS
AND OVER, 1986, 1996, 2006

Source: Statistics Canada, Families and Households, *2006 Census,* 97-553-XWE2006001,
September 2007; http://www.statcan.gc.ca/bsolc/olc-cel/olc-cel?catno=97-553-
XWE2006001&lang=eng

Canada's population aged 15 or over regarding marital status,
but you are also able to see the trend for the legally married
portion of the population.

WHERE TO PLACE GRAPHICS

Graphics should be placed wherever they'll be most useful.
They should not distract readers or disrupt the reading flow.
If a graphic is too large to be non-disruptive, place it in an
appendix at the back of your report.

Wherever you place the graphic, be sure to refer to it in
your text and point out to readers what they should notice in
the graphic.

EXPLORATIONS

10.1 In the library, locate a book of government statistics, or go to the Statistics Canada or another government website. Find a table, line chart, bar chart, and pie chart.

10.2 With a partner or in a small group, brainstorm and list situations from your field in which you would use each type of graphic.

10.3 Find examples of graphics in newspapers. Discuss whether newspapers use graphics differently from the way they are used in reports and presentations.

10.4 Choose any graphic in this chapter and discuss what you could learn from that graphic. What information could be gleaned from an analysis of the figure or table? What does the graphic tell you?

10.5 Using data from Table 10.3, create a bar chart for the number of shelters for abused women in your province or territory in 2007–2008.

Table 10.3

NUMBER OF SHELTERS FOR ABUSED WOMEN BY TYPE OF FACILITY, CANADA, PROVINCES AND TERRITORIES, 2007–2008

	Transition House	Second Stage Housing	Women's Emergency Centre	Emergency Shelter	Safe Home Network	Other[1]	Total, All Shelter Types	
			Number				Number	Rate[2]
Canada	**265**	**104**	**67**	**77**	**17**	**39**	**569**	**7**
Newfoundland and Labrador	6	4	1	2	0	2	15	11
Prince Edward Island	0	4	0	1	0	0	5	14
Nova Scotia	11	4	0	1	0	0	16	7
New Brunswick	14	4	0	2	1	1	22	12
Quebec	101	12	2	1	0	10	126	7
Ontario	49	29	20	47	0	15	160	5
Manitoba	3	7	6	5	1	7	29	11
Saskatchewan	8	6	3	6	0	1	24	10
Alberta	4	10	31	3	0	2	50	6
British Columbia	64	23	1	6	15	1	110	10
Yukon	2	1	1	1	0	0	5	65
Northwest Territories and Nunavut[3]	3	0	2	2	0	0	7	47

[1] Includes Ontario's Family Resource Centres, Manitoba's Interim housing, satellites, and other facilities not otherwise classified.

[2] Rates are calculated based on 100,000 population of married, common-law, and separated women. Separated includes persons currently married, but who are no longer living with their spouse (for any reason other than illness or work) and have not obtained a divorce. Persons who are separated but who live with a common-law partner are not included. Population estimates are provided by Statistics Canada, Demography Division. Populations as of July 1: preliminary post-censal estimates for 2007.

[3] Due to a limited number of facilities in conjunction with low response rates for Northwest Territories and Nunavut, information for shelters in these territories has been combined, for reasons of confidentiality and data quality.

Source: Source: Statistics Canada, Study: Family Violence and Shelters for Abused Women 2007, *The Daily*, 11-001-XIE, Thursday, October 15, 2009; http://www.statcan.gc.ca/daily-quotidien/091015/dq091015b-eng.htm

CHAPTER 11

MARKETING IN THE HUMAN SERVICES

Overview: This chapter discusses marketing in human services agencies, explaining the uses of marketing and methods of reaching the public.

WHY MARKET MY SERVICE?

An American manufacturer of baby food used to advertise its products with the slogan "Babies are our business—our only business." Community service agencies might rephrase that old slogan as "People are our business—our only business." Without clients, the agency cannot perform its function, which is, after all, helping clients. That's why agencies need to market—they need to reach people to be effective. An agency or centre that no one is aware of is failing to live up to its mandate as a human service organization.

WHO IS MY AUDIENCE?

Your target audience depends on your purpose. Do you want to be sure that other professionals are aware of your agency, so that they can make referrals? Do you want potential clients to be aware of your existence, so that they can self-refer?

Do you want companies and civic organizations to realize that your agency would be a worthy recipient of their charitable contributions? Do you want to reach potential individual donors?

If part of your mandate is education, is there a group you wish to reach, either with information or with an invitation to a specific function, such as a demonstration, lecture, or workshop?

HOW DO I MARKET?

This is the tough part, at first. However, the process of marketing the community service agency can be learned, and it can be enjoyable. It is important to remember that you are advertising your agency, and *advertising* is primarily a *visual medium*. It is essential that whatever brochures or flyers you produce be attractive visually. The steps below outline the details more fully, but be aware at the outset that whatever you produce must be pleasing to the eye.

MARKETING STEP ONE: SELECTING A MEDIUM

You are the director of a youth outreach service called Freedom, which deals with drug and alcohol addiction in youths aged 8 to 16. You do not do counselling; your mandate is to provide education and referral. Your catchment area is Sydney, Nova Scotia. The service has just opened, and your profile is so low as to be nonexistent. How do you make people aware of your agency?

First of all, whom do you want to be aware of your services (who is your target audience)?

- adolescents
- their parents
- their teachers
- other professionals

Different groups can be reached through different media. What are the options?

- *Newspapers:* Local or community newspapers are ideal for reaching a specific audience. Newspaper staff are always looking for human-interest or newsworthy material, so a call to the paper might lead to an article being written on your service. You might write an article on a general-interest topic related to your work. Many newspapers also have a community page where nonprofit groups can advertise free of charge. You could also place a classified ad in the personals section, but the first two options would be more likely to reach a wider audience.

- *Television:* Cable TV provides community channels where nonprofit groups can often advertise free of charge. As well, local breakfast television shows are often looking for interesting community content.

- *Letters:* Letters to community leaders, such as school principals, presidents of school PTAs, and religious leaders (notices can sometimes be placed free of charge in church bulletins)—all of these things can serve to introduce your service. You also need to introduce your agency to other professionals.

- *Presentations:* An open house, a presentation at a PTA meeting, or a talk at a lodge meeting are good ways to directly contact your audience. Giving a presentation at a professional conference is a powerful way to network and raise your agency's profile with your peers.

- *Brochures and flyers:* These can be effective methods of marketing, but how will you distribute them? Direct mailing on a wide scale is prohibitively expensive. An alternative, especially when dealing with a geographically defined area, is contracting for house-to-house delivery. You could also make use of community groups again, such as by delivering brochures to schools to be given to each student. Public libraries are also useful distribution points.

- *Internet:* The easiest way to reach many people today is online. Internet marketing will be discussed separately at the end of this chapter.

Let's say you decided to explore all these possibilities. You contacted the community paper, and a reporter will be interviewing you next week. You contacted the cable company, and they'll be running the following ad for you:

TEENS
Problems or questions about
alcohol or other drugs?

FREEDOM
can help. We're confidential.
Call us anytime.
(902) 622-5465

You also have written a semipersonalized letter to the school principals in the area (by semipersonalized I mean that each principal gets the same form letter, but with appropriate names and addresses changed so that it doesn't look like a form letter). The letter looks like this:

SEMIPERSONALIZED LETTER

```
FREEDOM
Youth Outreach Service
54 Mimico Avenue
Sydney, Nova Scotia

Dear:

FREEDOM is a community-based youth outreach service
dealing with drug and alcohol addiction in Sydney
youths aged 8 to 16. We do not do counselling, but
rather concentrate on education and referrals to
other agencies. We focus on drug and alcohol educa-
tion and are available to speak to students and to
community, parent, or religious groups. We are ready
to talk to groups of any size. Our presentations
are, of course, free of charge.
```

We also refer youths or families with addiction-related problems to appropriate agencies. Our service is confidential.

Please feel free to call on us at any time, either to book a presentation or to ask any questions you may have about our agency or about youth drug/alcohol use in Sydney. We have enclosed a brochure describing our agency. We would be happy to forward extra copies if you would like to distribute our brochures to your students.

Children in trouble need our help. Please introduce your students to FREEDOM.

Sincerely,

Jean Paul Gauthier
Director

You're sending the same letter to the schools' PTA presidents, and a slightly different letter to the religious leaders in the area, requesting that they mention the new service in a bulletin or in front of their congregation.

You're working on the letter announcing your agency to the professional community, and you are planning to ask some community groups if they would consider you as a guest speaker. What you need to work on immediately, though, is a brochure and a flyer to send out with all these letters.

Brochures and Flyers

What's the difference between a brochure and a flyer? A flyer, as I'm using the term, is a single sheet of paper, often meant to be posted, and always meant to attract attention and to convey a message almost instantaneously. A brochure might also be just one sheet of paper, but it is folded, contains more information, and takes a bit longer to read. Brochures for community service agencies are sometimes produced professionally, but agency staff can also create brochures themselves. The following are not the only styles of brochures, but they are probably the easiest:

- 8 1/2" × 11" sheet folded in half
- 8 1/2" × 14" sheet folded in three, two ends meeting in the middle
- 8 1/2" × 11" sheet folded in even thirds, the first third folded to the right and the last third folded to the middle, under the first

To see how each might look (imagine them folded), take a look at Figure 11.1.

MARKETING STEP TWO: WRITING COPY

You have chosen the third type of brochure style. Now you need to write your copy (compose the text of the brochure). Actually, you would never really think of the text separately; you must always consider, at the same time, how your ad will look. However, for the sake of simplicity let's talk just about text, or copy, for now.

You can't say everything. A good ad is an economical one—economical not just in terms of getting the most for your money, but also in getting the most for your words. Choose what is most important. What do you most want to tell people about your agency?

Figure 11.1

STYLES OF BROCHURES

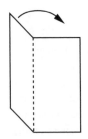 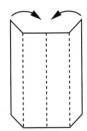 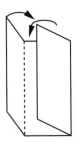

With a brochure, you must capture readers' attention, tell them a few significant things, and then let them go. In selecting what to put in the brochure, consider it from the reader's point of view: Does the reader really want or need to know this particular information? If yes, fine; otherwise, leave it out.

As you write, keep in mind the literacy level of your target audience. Don't be patronizing in your language, but remember that some of your readers may be functionally illiterate. Write clearly, simply, and concisely.

Let's assume you have decided on the information you want to convey in the brochure:

- the agency's name
- the agency's philosophy and mandate
- agency services
- agency hours
- agency location

Now you need to put that information into words—appealing words. Here's where you begin to think visually at the same time.

MARKETING STEP THREE: DESIGNING A BROCHURE

With the style of brochure you have chosen, you have six usable surfaces:

- page 1, actually the last third of the back of the sheet
- pages 2 through 4, each a third of the front of the sheet
- pages 5 and 6, the other two-thirds of the back of the sheet

Confused? Get out a sheet of paper, turn it 90 degrees, fold the last third to the left, then the first third to the right. Number the pages as indicated above.

On page 1 you want the *headline,* something to catch the reader's attention. Pages 2 through 4 could describe the agency's philosophy, mandate, and services. Page 5 could give the hours and phone number, and page 6 could contain a map giving your location in relation to a major intersection.

Figure 11.2 on page 136 shows how the brochure might look.

Figure 11.2

EXAMPLE OF A BROCHURE

How to Reach Us

We are located at
54 Mimico Avenue in
Sydney. You can drop in
any day between
9:00 a.m. and 9:00 p.m.
You can call us anytime,
day or night,
at **(902) 622-5465**.

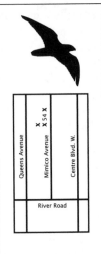

Queens Avenue

X
X 54 X

Mimico Avenue

Centre Blvd. W.

River Road

FREEDOM

YOUTH
OUTREACH
SERVICE

Who We Are

FREEDOM is a
community-based
youth outreach
service that deals
with drug and
alcohol addiction in
Sydney youths aged
8 to 16.

What We Do

FREEDOM focuses on
drug and alcohol
education. We are
available to speak to
school, community,
parent, and religious
groups of any size.
Our presentations are
free of charge.

We also refer youths
or families with
addiction-related
problems to
appropriate agencies.
Our service is
confidential.

DESIGNING A FLYER

As I mentioned, a flyer is designed for quick visual impact. Like the brochure, it consists of both headline and copy, but the copy is very brief.

When designing both the brochure and the flyer, it is useful to do a thumbnail sketch of the finished project. A thumbnail sketch of the flyer might look like the one shown in Figure 11.3.

Figure 11.3

THUMBNAIL SKETCH

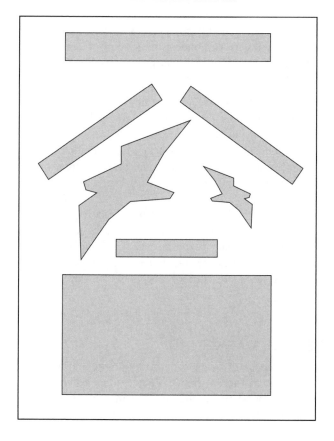

You work with the thumbnail sketch, moving things around, changing things until you like the look of the ad. Then you perfect each separate item by following these steps:

- write the headline
- write the copy
- prepare the illustrations
- do a "paste-up" of the finished ad, taping each item in place
- duplicate the ad, using a photocopier or professional printer, or create the flyer using a word-processing or presentation software program. These programs are easy to learn and manipulate.

Figure 11.4 on page 139 shows an example of a completed flyer, created using a common word-processing program and its "Insert picture" function. However you complete it, here are a few hints for designing a flyer:

- For visual interest, use *contrast*—different type sizes, different lines (diagonals, horizontals, verticals). Compose your ad as you would a painting.
- Remember that English-speakers read from left to right and from top to bottom; ensure that the order of the text or illustrations works with our natural reading tendencies.
- Be sure to leave plenty of white space (space where there is neither text nor illustration); the eye becomes fatigued if a page is too busy and if there is no white space for the eye to rest. But watch out for too much white space—it will look as though you have nothing to say!

INTERNET MARKETING

Many agencies, both for-profit and nonprofit, are using the Internet to reach their audience. People often search first on the Internet for whatever they are seeking, whether it be a new car, a new camera, or help they might need that a human

Figure 11.4

ARE YOU BETWEEN 8 AND 16?

DO YOU HAVE QUESTIONS ABOUT ALCOHOL OR DRUGS?

DO YOU HAVE DRUG OR ALCOHOL-RELATED PROBLEMS?

FREEDOM CAN HELP

We're a youth outreach service

Teaching about addictions
Making referrals
Listening when you need a friend

We're confidential

Give us a call, anytime, day or night

(902) 622-5465

services organization could provide. As we discussed in the research chapter, the most efficient way to find something on the Internet is to use a search engine.

Search engines reach their results by looking for meta-tags on web pages, sometimes called searchable text; in other words, the search engines are looking for keywords. When a match is found, the website is included in the search engine's results. The higher the degree of match, the higher on the results page the website is listed. Many people look at only the first page of results, or even only the first few offerings.

For an agency wanting to reach clients, this means that getting high up on that list by optimizing searchable text is key. Unless you have a background in web design, with an emphasis on this area, it's probably best to hire a web designer. Ending up on page two or three of the search results is useless.

A well-designed website is priceless. Not only can it reach clients, it can also be a powerful tool for advocacy and education. The emerging field of social marketing aims to harness the power of marketing, including Internet marketing, to influence individuals' behaviour to improve their well-being and that of society (http://www.social-marketing.org/aboutus.html).

EXPLORATIONS

11.1 Analyze three to five actual brochures or flyers for their effectiveness. Discuss their strong and weak points. Offer suggestions for improvement, if needed.

11.2 Advertise your daycare centre to the surrounding area. Prepare a brochure, a flyer, and a distribution plan for your advertising materials.

11.3 Prepare a parent handbook for your daycare centre.

11.4 If you have been assigned the funding-proposal project (see Chapter 5), prepare an advertising campaign to create awareness of your new agency or service. Prepare a letter to relevant community services or to other professionals who should be aware of your agency, as well as a brochure and, if appropriate, a flyer.

11.5 Advertise the following workshops and prepare a booklet to be distributed at each workshop:

a. a parenting workshop, covering discipline
b. an in-service workshop for elementary schoolteachers on mainstreaming students who are developmentally delayed
c. a workshop on kids and drugs for an elementary school or high-school PTA
d. a workshop for an advocacy group for persons with disabilities on providing travel opportunities for clients
e. a workshop for the community on home care of aging parents
f. a workshop for low-income pregnant mothers on nutrition during pregnancy
g. a workshop on the benefits of child life (recreational therapy) activities in a hospital setting for the hospital's Parent Committee
h. a workshop for travel agents on wilderness treks
i. a workshop for parents of children with learning disabilities on how summer camping can help their children's self-esteem
j. a workshop for workers in your field on stress management and avoiding burnout

11.6 Prepare a booklet for your group home/community-living residence entitled "Rules for Residents."

11.7 Prepare a brochure and/or letter to solicit funds for your organization.

11.8 Prepare a flyer for a fundraising yard sale.

11.9 Prepare a flyer for a fundraising bake sale.

11.10 You are a CYW in a local high school. Create a brochure or flyer to educate students about staying safe online.

11.11 Create a flyer advertising a lunch-and-learn series for staff.

11.12 Create a flyer advertising the reward and recognition program from Exploration 3.13 and a brochure explaining the program's procedures.

11.13 Create a flyer and handouts for a workshop on any of the topics in the Explorations in Chapter 7.

11.14 Go to the "Papers" section of the Social Marketing Institute website (http://www.social-marketing.org/papers.html) and read the proceedings of the 2000 Marketing Summit Conference to get an insight into social marketing.

11.15 Read the paper at the following link to see social marketing in action: http://www.experiencecorps.org/assets/Experience CorpsandSocialMarketing_AmericanJournalofPublicHealth. pdf.

CHAPTER 12

SPEAKING SKILLS IN THE HUMAN SERVICES

Overview: This chapter discusses oral presentation skills needed by community service workers. A community service professional some-times needs to speak in public as part of his or her educational or advocacy role. It is important, as always, to keep in mind the needs of the audience. This chapter also discusses the use of visual aids.

PUBLIC SPEAKING

You may be wondering why a community service professional has to worry about oral presentation skills. After all, you're not going into politics or the theatre. However, there will be times in your professional life when you will be speaking in front of an audience, even if that audience is a small one. Part of your role as a professional is to educate—your clients, your peers, or the larger community. Another part is acting as an advocate, either for individual clients or for a client group as a whole. You will also face unexpected occasions when you are expected to speak.

Few people enjoy public speaking. I personally can face a a root canal without the freezing with more fortitude and less anxiety than I can face speaking in public. My hands begin to tremble, my voice gets higher (I'm a soprano, so it's fairly high already), and I begin, not to perspire, but to sweat. I am not alone in this. Notice how many speakers keep their hands in their pockets!

Granted, you may not enjoy speaking in public, but you can survive it without making a fool of yourself. *Just concentrate on your message and on your audience's need to hear it.*

Don't think of yourself. Think of the message. If you don't tell your audience what they need to hear, perhaps no one will. Think of how important your message is. Even if your hands do shake and your voice does quaver, at least the audience will hear what you have to say. As well, you may be surprised to find that, once you get started, it does get easier to go on.

What are the steps in preparing a speech? First of all, consider purpose and audience. What do you want your speech to do? What is your audience like? What is their attitude and level of knowledge about your topic now? What is their probable reaction to you? How can you establish your credibility? How can you get their attention?

Consider constraints of time and space. How long will you be speaking? Don't try to cram too much into a short space of time. Consider the room you'll be speaking in. Is it comfortable? Will your listeners start to shift after a few minutes on hard chairs or benches? Focus on what you most want to tell your audience.

Then organize. How can you most effectively get your message across? Prepare an outline, being sure to include examples and anecdotes that will be relevant to your audience. Remember that listeners' attention sometimes wanders. Make it simple, so that a returning listener won't be totally lost, but don't talk down to your audience. Respect them, or you really will be all alone up there.

Rehearse your speech, timing yourself and including visual aids. When it's showtime, take some cleansing breaths (it works for having a baby, but that may be easier), then get in there and deliver your message.

Here are a few basic rules to follow in giving a speech:

1. *Be prepared, but not overprepared.* Know your material, so that you are comfortable with it, but do not write out a complete speech. If you have a complete speech written out, the temptation is to read it, which is deadly. Never read a speech. Speak to your audience, don't read at them.

If you are well prepared, you can sound spontaneous, paradoxical as that may seem.

2. *Look at your audience as you speak.* In this culture, it is customary to look at the person you are speaking to. What do we say about someone who doesn't? "He couldn't look me in the eye." It is essential to maintain eye contact when speaking. Don't look over people's heads, don't look down at the floor, and don't stare at your visual aids—look at your audience. Think of your speech as a conversation. You would look at the other person then, wouldn't you? Looking at your audience personalizes your speech and, usually, makes it more interesting.

3. *Speak loudly enough to be heard clearly, and use a natural pitch.* You aren't calling hogs, so you needn't bellow, but at the same time you must be sure to be heard. You may have a lovely, delicate voice, but if it doesn't carry past the second row you need to pump up the volume. People can't get your message if they can't hear it. At the same time, watch your pitch. Try to sound natural. Watch out for sounding tentative. In English, we raise the pitch of our voices at the end of a question; when making a statement, the pitch goes down. Say these two sentences out loud:

> "Is that the book you borrowed from Kathy?"
>
> "I borrowed that book from Kathy."

Notice the difference? What happens if your voice rises in pitch at the end of a statement? You sound like you're asking a question, which translates into sounding tentative and unsure of yourself. Do it enough and you sound as though you're asking for approval, or else as though you don't really know what you're talking about. Watch your pitch.

4. *Speak slowly, but with enthusiasm.* Don't hyperventilate by rushing your speech out and setting a new record. Slow

down. Slowing down helps to overcome your nervousness, and it certainly makes listening to your speech easier on your audience. Don't slow to a crawl, though. Be enthusiastic. Be real. Be careful not to speak in a monotone, putting everyone, including yourself, to sleep. And be sure to smile.

5. *Stand or sit comfortably, but don't slouch.* Don't touch your hair, don't drum your fingers on the table, don't rock back and forth, and don't touch your face. One of my students, an amateur boxer, gave a speech once and kept rubbing the bottom of his nose with his hand (the way fighters do while getting ready to land a punch). Unfortunately, from where I was sitting, it looked like he was picking his nose. Keep those hands away from the face!

There is one thing you should never do. *Never apologize.* You are doing the best job you can, and it's probably a good one. You know what you're talking about, and your audience needs to hear you; apologizing only undermines your credibility. Besides, there's not a person in the audience who would trade places with you. You're doing fine.

Before I discuss visual aids, just a word about questions. When you finish the speech, you breathe a sigh of relief, but then someone raises a hand. Just when you thought you were finished, there are questions. How do you handle questions?

Clearly, briefly, and simply. Look at the person who asked the question. Unless the questioner had a booming voice, repeat the question so everyone hears it, and then look at the whole audience and answer *briefly.* You already gave a speech, and there's no need to give another one. What if you don't know the answer? Say so. Don't bluff, just admit that you can't answer a particular question, but say that you'll try to get the answer. People respect honesty. No one knows or remembers everything.

What if someone asks a silly question, or one that you've already answered? *Never make fun of a question or the person asking it.* Not only is that unkind, it's suicidal. The audience will turn on you. You will then either get really hard questions that no one could possibly answer, or else everyone will be afraid to ask a question for fear of being ridiculed. Either way, you'll have lost the audience.

VISUAL AIDS

"Visual aid" is a catch-all term that covers anything that visually helps to get across your message, from handouts to a live baby in a baby bath demonstration. The most common visual aids are

1. *Handouts.* Consider carefully the timing of "handing out" your handouts. Unless you want the audience to be able to follow along on their handouts, keep all written material until the end of your presentation. Why? What do you do when you're handed reading material? Chances are you read it. Most people aren't good at reading and listening at the same time. So if you want your audience to listen to you, hang on to the handouts until the end. The exception is if you've prepared handouts of PowerPoint slides with spaces for notes. Having your audience jot down a few thoughts as you speak just might keep them engaged throughout your talk.

2. *Whiteboard/flip chart.* Be neat. Be sure people can read what you write. And be sure not to talk to the board or the chart, but to your audience. Also, make sure you're not standing in the way, blocking out the board or chart your audience is trying to read.

3. *PowerPoints.* PowerPoints are the most common visual aid today, but don't get carried away with the technology. I have seen some lovely high-tech presentations that were hollow at the core. The presenter had paid more attention to the flashy medium than to the message. Presentation software is a tool that aids in the delivery of your message, as long as you do not become mesmerized by the technology. Focus on the essence of what you need to communicate, letting the technology complement your message rather than obscure it. One final caution: technology sometimes breaks down. Be prepared with a backup plan in case your equipment malfunctions, as it sometimes will do when it's most needed. (See below for PowerPoint tips.)

Always rehearse with your visual aids so that they fit in smoothly. Above all, don't let them get in the way of your message or your rapport with the audience. Talk to your audience, not to the visual aid.

CREATING EFFECTIVE POWERPOINT PRESENTATIONS

The following discussion summarizes material that can be found at this website:

http://www.ensc.sfu.ca/resources/technical/writing/effective_ presentation.ppt

When creating a PowerPoint presentation (or overhead transparencies), look at things from the audience's perspective. It is essential that the audience be able to read your slides with ease. Here are a few tips from the author of the above presentation:

- Keep it big: pick a font that is large enough for your audience to read from where they're sitting.
- Keep it simple: apply the 6 × 7 rule—no more than 6 lines per slide and no more than 7 words per line.
- Keep it clear:
  - Use a mixture of upper and lower case. All capital letters are hard to read on a slide.
  - Use a **sans serif** font. This book is printed in a serif font, with decorative strokes on the letters. A sans serif font has clean lines and is easier to read on a slide.
  - Avoid italics. Italicized words are harder to read on a slide.
  - Use normal or **bold** type for clarity.
  - Avoid underlining. Underlining is used to indicate a hyperlink to a web page.
  - Use bulleted or numbered lists to improve clarity.

Another useful guide can be found at this website: http:// www.slideshare.net/thecroaker/death-by-powerpoint

EXPLORATIONS

12.1 Offer one of the following presentations in the format (individual, group) and length set by your teacher:

    a. nutrition during pregnancy (audience: lower income pregnant women)

    b. mainstreaming students who are developmentally delayed (audience: elementary schoolteachers)

    c. mainstreaming students who are developmentally delayed (audience: parent association)

    d. benefits of child life activities in a hospital setting (audience: hospital budget committee)

    e. sexuality in the developmentally delayed teenager (audience: parents)

    f. the group home in the community (audience: ratepayers group)

    g. survival camping: pushing the envelope at spring break (audience: college student association executive)

    h. handling the terrible twos (audience: parents)

    i. enhancing children's creativity through games (audience: parents)

    j. summer camping for students with learning disabilities as a help to self-esteem (audience: local parent meeting of Learning Disabilities Association)

    k. caring for an aging parent at home (audience: primary caregivers)

    l. travel opportunities for travellers with disabilities (audience: advocacy group for disabled persons)

    m. the future of our profession (audience: your peers)

    n. reasons for instituting a reward and recognition program in your agency (audience: upper management)

    o. enjoying social networking safely (audience: teens)

    p. social networking guidelines in the workplace (audience: co-workers at your organization)

    q. any topic from the Explorations in Chapter 7 (assume appropriate audience)

12.2 The project for which you submitted a funding proposal has been placed on a short list of candidates for new program funding. There is a short list of seven; only three new programs can be funded. All seven candidates have been asked to give a brief presentation before the committee that will make the final decision on which three programs will receive funding. Make that presentation, convincing the committee to fund your program.

12.3 Read any article you find interesting in a professional journal. Imagine you have heard the article presented as a workshop at a professional conference. At a staff meeting, report to your colleagues what you learned at the workshop.

12.4 Summarize a client's progress at an IPRC meeting.

12.5 Summarize a client's progress at a client review meeting.

12.6 Simulate a staff meeting in an agency in your field, with different members of your group taking on various roles. Have one member act as observer, taking notes on the roles people have assumed and on interactions during the meeting. As a group, discuss the mock meeting afterward and identify strengths, weaknesses, and characteristics of the roles and interactions.

12.7 A one-on-one meeting with a client can also be considered a presentation, since you are both "presenting" yourselves to each other. With a partner and using a digital camcorder, if possible, role-play a worker–client interaction that goes badly, perhaps because of poor presentation skills on either side, and one that goes well. Immediately afterward, discuss your reactions to the other person's language, including body language. Switch roles and role-play a follow-up meeting. Be creative in inventing the topic of the initial interaction. (Additional suggestion: perhaps you could pause after the "bad" interaction and have the class or your group discuss what went wrong. Use their suggestions in your "good" interaction.)

CHAPTER 13

Overview: This chapter provides an introduction to the job-search process in the human services field.

KNOWING YOUR SKILLS

We have been looking at communication tasks in the human services field—situations you may be facing in the future when on the job. Of course, these days the most difficult task may be getting that job in the first place. Funding cutbacks, downsizing—all those added pressures have made the job search even more daunting than in the past.

Chances are that you will not immediately, or perhaps even ultimately, get a job in the exact area for which you trained. Child and youth workers may work with senior citizens, developmental services workers with troubled youth, or social service workers in a recreational setting. As well, few people these days retire in the job or the field in which they began. It is a truism to talk about change being the only constant, but truisms have that name for a reason. Fields change, jobs change, and we change. What remains? *Generic skills*.

Generic skills are the skills that are common to all fields and that enable one to learn and thrive in the midst of change. Generic skills are usually broken down into such areas as communication skills, numeracy or math skills, computer or technology skills, analytical or critical thinking skills, interpersonal skills, research skills, and the skill of learning to learn, of being a self-directed learner.

Throughout your college career you have not only learned the skills of your field, or *vocational skills,* but you have also been developing generic skills that will aid you no matter what your ultimate career. Indeed, this textbook is grounded in generic skills instruction. Were you to switch from the human services field to any other career, the generic skills you have been practising would be transferable to that new field.

What does all of this have to do with finding a job? Plenty. When employers are asked what they are looking for in considering job applicants, a common theme is "generic skills." Employers often go on to say that they are ready and able to teach new hires the specific vocational skills needed for a given job, as long as those new employees possess the following generic skills: communication skills, the ability to work as part of a team, and a readiness to take responsibility for their professional development and to continue to learn on the job.

Job applicants are sometimes surprised to find that they are expected to take a math test or to do a writing assessment before they will be considered for a position. Applicants with excellent vocational skills are sometimes eliminated from consideration because they fail these prescreening exercises.

WRITING A RÉSUMÉ

The prescreening begins with the employer's analysis of the applicant's résumé and cover letter. In this job market, employers receive hundreds of résumés for each position. Clearly, an employer cannot interview every applicant and, thus, must sort the résumés of those to be interviewed from those to be sent a polite rejection letter. Many of the applicants will have similar credentials. How can you stand out against the competition?

Let's start by mentioning how not to stand out. I have prescreened thousands of résumés, and I am always surprised at the elementary mistakes some applicants make. I have seen and rejected résumés that

- were handwritten in pencil
- were written on lined loose-leaf paper
- spelled the name of my college incorrectly
- spelled my name incorrectly
- contained spelling mistakes
- contained grammatical errors
- contained typing errors
- applied to a different organization (i.e., the résumés got in the wrong envelopes)

Keep in mind that I was usually hiring for positions teaching writing, sometimes even résumé writing. Clearly, the applicants making the above mistakes had totally misread their audience and were defeating their purpose! However, most employers would reject out of hand résumés that made the above mistakes, no matter what the job, because these errors display a lack of care and attention to detail that employers, rightly or wrongly, assume will carry over into job responsibilities. The résumé writer has damaged his or her credibility as a professional through sloppiness and inattention.

What happens to such résumés? They quickly move to the reject pile.

How do you avoid such a fate? Through careful attention to purpose and audience. What is your purpose in sending a résumé and cover letter? To get an interview. Who is your audience? A manager who is overworked and who sees hundreds of résumés, but who sincerely wishes to hire the best person for the job. He or she is looking for someone with the right mix of vocational knowledge and generic skills to make a contribution to the organization. Your task, then, is to convince the manager that you are that person.

APPLYING FOR SOLICITED
AND UNSOLICITED POSITIONS

Let's begin with the first stages of your job search. There are two types of job applications: solicited and unsolicited. In this job market, you likely need to send out both types.

Solicited applications are those sent in response to an advertisement or job posting. The organization or agency is actively looking for someone for a specific position. You might find the ad in the want ads or career section of your local paper, at your school's job placement centre, in "positions" sections of professional journals, or even on the Internet. In sending a solicited application, you would tailor your cover letter, and perhaps even your résumé, to the advertised position.

Many organizations now do *keyword searches* on résumés and cover letters. Automated programs search the application for keywords from the job posting, so it's more important than ever to tailor your application to the advertised position. The posting will have listed job duties and qualifications; be sure to respond directly to the posting, echoing keywords, or risk being screened out before a human being even has a chance to see your application. *(Note: Some organizations require you to fill out or submit an online application; the same rule of hitting the keywords applies in that situation as well.)*

Unsolicited applications are those sent out "on spec," in hopes of being kept in mind for any current or future openings. I was hired as a result of an unsolicited application, and I have hired many fine teachers as a result of their sending résumés on spec. Unsolicited applications may lead to an interview, to a part-time or contract position, and then to full-time work when something suitable arises. The whole point is to become known. *To know you is to love you, after all, but first you need to get in the door.*

Just as with a solicited application, unsolicited applications require prior research. You need to seek out agencies and organizations that might be a good fit for your skills. Again, in this job market, you might want to cast your net widely and consider fields related to your specialty that might be suitable. Do a skills inventory. What aptitudes and abilities do you have that might cross the boundaries between fields? What are you good at? (Look at other job markets besides the obvious. For example, you may have an early childhood education diploma, but how about being a child life worker in a children's hospital?)

Most, if not all, urban centres have a listing of agencies and organizations that provide social and community services in the region. Look through the listing for agencies that you find interesting and that might be suitable places to send your résumé. Then continue to do some homework. Who at the agency should receive your résumé? Give the agency a call to ask for a name, and be sure to get the spelling, along with the correct form of address (Mrs., Ms., Dr., and so on) and the job title.

Find out just what the agency does and if it has a specific theoretical orientation. Is it a Montessori daycare? Does the agency work from an Adlerian perspective? If you can, get a copy of its mission statement and guiding principles. Some organizations may give only lip service to their stated mission and principles, but others follow that mission in every task and expect all employees to share commitment to that mission. Does the organization seem like a place where you would be happy and fulfilled?

Finally, use all this information in crafting your cover letter and in customizing your résumé. In the age of word processing, it is easy to customize job application packages, and therefore there is little excuse for sending exactly the same résumé and cover letter to each agency.

Let's look at the sample résumé below.

SAMPLE RÉSUMÉ

```
                    Derrick Fallion
                    11 Ardwick Avenue, Apt. 412
                    Toronto, Ontario
                    (416) 333-5555
                    fallion345@hotmail.com
```

Education

Centennial College   2009–2011
Toronto, Ontario
Diploma in Recreation and Leisure Services

Field Placement Experience

Brentwood Seniors Home   September 2010–April 2011
Toronto, Ontario
Responsible for planning and implementing recre-
ational activities for groups of senior citizens.

Parks and Recreation   January 2010–April 2010
Toronto, Ontario
Responsible for implementing planned recreational
activities at community centre locations.

Work Experience

Parks and Recreation   March 2006–present
Toronto, Ontario
Certified lifeguard, with Bronze Cross. Moved from
trainee to head lifeguard.

Volunteer Experience

North York Lacrosse Association   2007–present
Central Arena
Timekeeper
Statistician
Coach of Novice Lacrosse House League

```
Bullets Hockey                        2008-present
Central Arena
Assistant Coach

Boy Scouts                            2008-present
Wolf Cub Pack Leader


Extracurricular Activities
_____

Student Associ ation                    2009-2011

Centennial Colts Hockey Team             2009-2011


References
_____

Available on request
```

Suppose Derrick is applying for a permanent position in Parks and Recreation, as arena manager at Central Arena. He probably would not need to make any changes to his basic résumé. The information he has already included and the manner of presentation would work well in applying for such a job.

In his cover letter, Derrick needs to emphasize what he has to offer that might place him ahead of other applicants. Certainly, his ongoing relationship with Central Arena as a volunteer is a plus. He might also point to his extensive volunteer work with young people, as well as to his increasing assumption of authority as he moved from trainee lifeguard to head lifeguard. As well, his educational background in recreation and leisure services would serve him well in this position.

What might his cover letter look like? Take a look below for an example.

SAMPLE COVER LETTER

11 Ardwick Avenue, Apt. 412
Toronto, Ontario

June 5, 2011

Matthew Foster, Director
Parks and Recreation
1752 Stanley Avenue
Toronto, Ontario

Dear Mr. Foster:

I am applying for the position of Arena Manager, Central Arena, advertised in the Toronto Star on June 3, 2011. I have long-standing ties to Central Arena, having played hockey and lacrosse there as a young man, and having volunteered as a coach in both sports in recent years, as well as serving as timekeeper and statistician.

I have worked with children and young people for many years. Besides coaching hockey and lacrosse, I have been a Scout leader with a Wolf Cub troop. I have excellent rapport with young people and enjoy coaching, teaching, and supporting them in their athletic and recreational activities.

I have worked as a lifeguard for many years, moving from trainee to head lifeguard. I hold a Bronze Cross and am trained in first aid and CPR. Finally, my education in recreation and leisure services has provided me with the skills to act as a recreation professional. I have a background in recreation pro-gramming and have developed strong interpersonal, team-building, and communication skills through my education and field placements. I am proficient in word processing and spreadsheet packages, and I used a database as statistician for the lacrosse and hockey associations.

I am available at your convenience for an interview. I can be reached at (416) 333-5555 or fallion345@ hotmail.com. I check for messages periodically throughout the day if I am not at home.

Sincerely,

Derrick Fallion

Derrick Fallion

Some applicants use coloured, marbled, or other specialty paper to make their résumés stand out. Some employers like that; some don't. Some applicants scan a photograph of themselves into their résumé. I personally do not like the practice. I have found that it distracts hiring committees, and it is not always to the candidate's advantage, no matter how attractive the picture. However, this may be a bias on my part.

"This may be a bias on my part." That sentence is significant, because it reveals that employers are human beings with human foibles, likes, and dislikes. For example, I dislike résumés that include a "Job Objective" at the top, and I have steeled myself to ignore my initial bias against résumés that include it; I know other people who like this category and are drawn to favour such résumés. How do you know whether the person getting your résumé likes or dislikes "Job Objective"? You don't. Anticipating your audience's reaction can go only so far. In the end, all you can do is do your homework, make it look good, and hope for the best.

To sum up, keep these important tips in mind when putting together your résumé and cover letter:

- Use good-quality paper.
- Change your ink cartridge if the imprint is not crisp and clear.
- Choose a readable font, and don't get cute by using script fonts—most people find them annoying.
- Leave plenty of white space, setting up the page so that it is attractive to the eye. (Remember, a résumé is an advertisement—you're selling yourself—and advertising is a visual medium.)
- List education and work experience in reverse chronological order, with the most recent first.
- Ask not what the agency can do for you (don't be "me-centred"); instead, focus on what you have to offer the organization.
- Proofread, proofread, proofread!

A note on social networking (or: be careful what you share!)

Many employers now make it a practice to check out applicants' social networking sites (SNS) as part of the screening process. You may feel that what you post on an SNS is private, but think again. The Privacy Commission of Canada warns, "Employees should know that SNS information may seem transitory and informal, but once personal information is posted online it gains permanence—and can be circulated and searched by others" (http://www.priv.gc.ca/fs-fi/02_05_d_41_sn_e.cfm). So be careful what you share. It's great to hang out, connect, and have fun, but what's posted online can come back to haunt you. Take a look at Explorations 13.6 and 13.7. Even if your instructor does not assign Exploration 13.7, it's a good idea to complete the exercise for your own protection.

THE INTERVIEW

The aim of the résumé is to get an interview. A good résumé can let you get your foot in the door. To get the rest of the way into an organization, you need a smashing interview.

So how do you prepare for a successful interview? Much the same way you prepared for a good résumé—research.

I still remember the interview that got me my faculty teaching position, and a closing question the selection committee chair asked: "How did you know just what we wanted?" It was really a rhetorical question, but the answer would have been simple. I studied the college before applying. I checked out its programs, its values, and its perception of itself as an institution. I thought about what I could offer this school. What in my education and experience made me a "good fit" for this college? Why was I the perfect candidate? And why was this college the perfect place for me?

It might seem a bit simpler to research a college than other institutions. After all, colleges publish lots of marketing material. Indeed, my first step was to get a college calendar, listing all the college's programs, its policies, and so on.

But most organizations have some material available to the public. Daycare centres, recreation centres, seniors' centres—all have some sort of marketing material. Group homes and public agencies have mission statements. Many organizations have websites. Learn what you can before your interview.

In addition, prepare yourself for some common questions. While all interviews are different, some questions are old standbys. Even if you don't face them in this interview, chances are you'll run into some of them someday, so prepare now. Here are some common interview questions:

- Tell us about your strengths and weaknesses. (Definitely a question you don't want to answer cold!)
- Tell us about a time you discovered an error in your work. What did you do in that situation?
- Tell us about a time you dealt with a conflict in the workplace. What actions did you take to resolve the issue or situation?
- Tell us about a time you worked as part of a team. What was the situation, what challenges did the team face, and how did you contribute to the team's success?
- Why are you suited to this position? What will you bring to it?
- Where do you see yourself in 10 years' time?
- Are there any questions you have for us?

These are a few standard questions. From your research, think about other questions you might face.

During the interview, be sure to make eye contact. Although you will probably be nervous, try to speak with confidence. Listen carefully, and don't be afraid to have a question repeated or clarified. Speak loudly enough to be heard and try to maintain a reasonable speaking pace, neither too fast nor too slow. Smile. Often at the end of an interview you will be asked if you have any questions. Be sure to prepare one or two intelligent, relevant questions in advance. Again, it is a chance to show you did your homework about the organization and to show your sincere interest in their work.

Much of the time, you will be interviewed by one person or by a small group. You might, however, someday face a larger selection committee, especially in the public sector or government-funded agencies. In my former college, a typical selection committee might have 10 to 12 members—a bit of a shock, if the interviewee isn't expecting such a crowd. It's okay to ask up front about who'll be doing the interviewing.

Just a word about barrier-free hiring. In a barrier-free hiring system, often the interviews are quite formal and scripted. The same questions are asked of all candidates, and there may be little or no use of follow-up probing questions. Again, this can be a surprise if the interviewee is expecting a less scripted interview, one based on his or her unique circumstances rather than one consisting of set questions, the "correct" answers to which may have been predetermined.

The idea behind barrier-free interviewing is to offer all candidates a level playing field, so don't be put off or alienated by this particular style of interviewing if you face it. The aim is still to display your talents and to convince the interviewers that you're the ideal candidate for the position. So whatever the format, be prepared, be confident, and you'll likely be successful.

And if you're not the successful candidate, be gracious. You may be interviewed by these folks again—burn no bridges. Treat the outcome as a learning experience. Often, if asked, interviewers are happy to share their insights on your performance with you. While a job interview can be stressful and an unsuccessful interview disappointing, many people have parlayed a rejection for one job into an offer for an even better job because they were willing to learn from the experience.

EXPLORATIONS

13.1 Do a job skills inventory. What particular skills do you have? What knowledge, specialized training, or aptitudes? List those skills, and then consider how those skills might be marketed to an employer. (Hand in this Exploration in the format requested by your teacher, such as journal entry or memo.)

13.2 Find an ad or a posting for a position in which you might be interested, either now or in the future. Prepare a résumé and cover letter to apply for that position.

13.3 Prepare an unsolicited résumé and cover letter for a position in a specific agency or organization.

13.4 Take a look at future opportunities in your profession. What might the situation be in 10 years? in 15? What type of further education or training might you need to be competitive in the future in your profession? Report back in a brief oral presentation, a journal entry, or a memo report.

13.5 With a partner, role-play a mock interview for the position you found in Exploration 13.2.

13.6 Watch the videos at the following links: http://www.youtube.com/watch?v=ualhXe_nT4k&feature=relatedf; http://www.youtube.com/watch?v=k2Kzw9me_fo&feature=related.

13.7 Evaluate your Facebook or other social networking page from an employer's perspective. What needs to change?

APPENDIX A

WHY ARE PROPER GRAMMAR AND PUNCTUATION IMPORTANT?

After all, you're not an English teacher, right? Who cares where the apostrophes go?

I could talk about an educated person's responsibility to use language well, or about the joy that articulate communication can bring, but I'll stick to pragmatism. Proper grammar and punctuation are important because other people judge you by your language, both oral and written. They make assumptions about you as a person and as a professional based on your language. This may not be fair, but it is reality. To demonstrate this tendency to students, I sometimes give them a copy of a real memo that is poorly written. The mistakes it contains run the gamut from run-on sentences to apostrophe errors to misspelled words and proofreading errors. After having the class determine what the writer wants as a result of this memo, I ask them why he will be unsuccessful. They point out the memo's failings. I then ask whether they think the writer is good at his actual (non-writing) job. It is the rare student who is willing to give him the benefit of the doubt. Many think that he should be fired, because if he's this sloppy in a memo, he must be doing a poor job the rest of the time. I know the writer personally, and he is intelligent, hardworking, and conscientious. The point is, however, that because his written communication skills are poor and his grammar and punctuation are slapdash, he comes across as stupid and lazy on paper.

If you wish to be accepted as a professional, you must write like a professional. People will not have confidence in your professional skills if your writing is substandard. The bottom line is that proper grammar and punctuation are important because mistakes in those areas reflect upon your professional competence.

The following is a brief review of a few points of grammar and punctuation. If you are weak in grammar, punctuation, or spelling, your teacher might suggest a suitable text to improve your skills.

THE BASICS

Let's start with the building blocks of sentences: parts of speech. There are eight parts of speech:

    a. nouns
    b. verbs
    c. adjectives
    d. adverbs
    e. prepositions
    f. conjunctions
    g. articles
    h. interjections

Here is a brief description of each of these:

    a. **Nouns** can be classified in several ways:
- proper (the proper names of things, e.g., Saskatchewan, Lucy, Ottawa Renegades) and common (the class of objects, e.g., person, province, team)
- concrete (objects, e.g., table, clock, house) and abstract (concepts, e.g., love, justice, peace)
- count (things that can be counted, e.g., knife, finger, tree) and non-count (things that can't be counted, e.g., sugar, air, music)

    b. **Verbs** can also be thought of in different ways:
- verbs are either transitive (taking an object, e.g., hit the ball), intransitive (not taking an object, e.g., sneeze), or copulative (sometimes called linking, e.g., is, seems)

- verbs have four principal parts (*base form or infinitive*, e.g., to sing, to play; *past*, e.g., sang, played; *past participle*, e.g., sung, played; *present participle*, e.g., singing, playing)
- verbs have different forms, depending on

  i. tense
      - present (talk)
      - past (talked)
      - future (will talk)
      - present perfect (have talked)
      - past perfect (had talked)
      - future perfect (will have talked)
      - present progressive (am talking)
      - past progressive (was talking)
      - future progressive (will be talking)
      - present perfect progressive (have been talking)
      - past perfect progressive (had been talking)
      - future perfect progressive (will have been talking)

  ii. person (first: I, we; second: you; third: he, she, it, they)

  iii. number (singular, plural)

  iv. mood (indicative: making a statement; imperative: giving a command;   subjunctive: hypothetical situations, situations contrary to fact, and so on)

  v. voice (active: the subject of the sentence performs the action; passive: the subject of the sentence is acted upon)

c. **Adjectives** modify nouns or pronouns
d. **Adverbs** modify verbs, adjectives, and adverbs
e. **Prepositions** are used in prepositional phrases to signal time (after the game), space (under the car), or direction (to the lighthouse)
f. **Conjunctions** are used to join words, phrases, or clauses; they come in two flavours: coordinating and subordinating (see page 169)

---

g. **Articles** come before nouns; there are two types:
   - definite (the): points to specific object (the table, the house, the old woman)
   - indefinite (a, an): points to generic object (a table, a house, an old woman)
h. **Interjections** are words or phrases interjected (tossed into) a sentence to express emotion (e.g., Yikes! Ouch! Oh dear!)

Why Are Parts of Speech Important?

Parts of speech are the building blocks of sentences. While one can certainly frame a sentence without knowing the names of parts of speech, it is difficult to eliminate errors if you lack a vocabulary that your teacher and other educated persons take for granted. It's hard to stop writing fragments, for instance, if you don't understand when your teacher tells you you're missing a verb. While it doesn't often come up in day-to-day conversation, the ability to identify and understand parts of speech is a useful skill, and critical to error-free writing.

Basics of Sentence Structure

The base structure of all sentences is quite simple: noun or pronoun plus verb. This basic structure is referred to as subject plus predicate.

$$N + V$$

or

$$P + V$$

In some cases, the subject does not even need to be stated, but instead is understood.

Listen!

(You) listen!

This base structure is an independent clause (IC). An independent clause can stand alone. It might be dull, it might be boring, but it is grammatically correct. A dependent clause (DC), on the other hand, cannot stand alone. It needs to be joined somehow to an independent clause if the sentence is to be grammatically correct.

Let's look at the following sentence:

> I went to the store.

"I" is the subject, "went" is the verb (or predicate), and "to the store" is a prepositional phrase modifying the verb (telling where I went).

Suppose I want to give more information. Why did I go to the store?

> I went to the store. I was out of milk.

This is correct, but it sounds childish. These two sentences can be combined with a conjunction.

> I went to the store because I was out of milk.

"Because" is a *subordinating conjunction*, making the part of the sentence it introduces dependent on the rest of the sentence for its meaning. Look what happens if I try to let that part of the sentence stand alone.

> Because I was out of milk.

Well? What happened because I was out of milk? What did I do because I was out of milk? The dependent clause makes little sense by itself; it requires the rest of the sentence for its meaning to be clear. (This type of error is called a *fragment*, since it is an incomplete sentence.)

Another type of conjunction is a *coordinating conjunction*. "Co" means equal; the two parts of a sentence joined by a coordinating conjunction could exist by themselves and still make sense.

> I was out of milk and I went to the store.

"And" is a coordinating conjunction (the others are *but*, *for*, *so*, and *yet*).

How about this sentence?

I was out of milk; therefore, I went to the store.

"Therefore" is not a conjunction but something called a *conjunctive adverb*. It does show the logical connection between two parts of a sentence, but it does not have the grammatical power to join them by itself; it requires a semicolon to finish the job. If I were to write

---

I was out of milk, therefore, I went to the store.

I would have written a *comma splice:* two sentences masquerading as one.

Sentence Types

There are four sentence types:

    a. A **simple** sentence consists of one independent clause, that is, a subject and a verb, along with any associated modifiers or prepositional phrases.

IC

I spoke to Juerg's sister yesterday.

---

    b. A **compound** sentence consists of two or more independent clauses joined by a coordinating conjunction.

IC coordinating conjunction IC

I spoke to Juerg's sister yesterday, but I haven't seen her today.

---

    c. A **complex** sentence consists of a dependent clause plus an independent clause. The dependent clause may include a subordinating conjunction.

DC, IC

> Although I haven't seen Juerg in weeks, I spoke to his sister yesterday.

or
IC, DC

> I spoke to Juerg's sister yesterday, although I haven't seen him in weeks.

d. A **compound-complex** sentence is a combination of the two types, consisting of one or more dependent clauses and one or more independent clauses.

DC, IC coordinating conjunction IC

> Although I haven't seen Juerg in weeks, I spoke to his sister yesterday, and she said he was fine.

or
IC coordinating conjunction IC, DC

> I spoke to Juerg's sister yesterday, but I haven't seen her today because she went out of town.

Subject–Verb Agreement

A singular subject takes a singular verb; a plural subject takes a plural verb.

> The *boy rides* his bike.
>
> The *boys ride* their bikes.

Notice that a verb in third-person singular ends in *s*. (I ride, you ride, he rides, we ride, you ride, they ride.)

Pronouns such as *everyone, everybody, anyone, someone,* and *somebody* are considered singular.

Pronoun Agreement

A pronoun stands for a noun (its antecedent). A singular antecedent takes a singular pronoun; a plural antecedent takes a plural pronoun (boy—his; boys—their).

The tricky part here is dealing with the indefinite pronouns that are considered singular, mentioned under subject–verb agreement. Technically speaking, the following sentence is correct:

> Everyone should bring his own paper to the test.

In speaking, however, we commonly use a plural possessive pronoun for these indefinite pronouns. In writing, a singular pronoun is still correct, but for how long is anyone's guess.

PUNCTUATION

Apostrophe

Another common source of errors is apostrophes. Some people sprinkle apostrophes liberally in their writing, letting them fall where they may, whereas others leave them out altogether. Neither practice is correct.

The apostrophe has two uses: to form *contractions* and to show *possession*.

> **Contractions:**
> would not—wouldn't
> do not—don't
> cannot—can't
> you are—you're
> it is—it's

Notice that the apostrophe in a contraction is placed wherever letters have been dropped. It is not placed haphazardly but, instead, stands for the missing letters.

> **Possession:**
> the coat belonging to the boy—the boy's coat
> the coats belonging to the boys—the boys' coats
> the coats belonging to them—their coats
> the fur belonging to the cat—the cat's fur
> the fur belonging to it (the cat)—its fur

Notice that possessive pronouns do not take an apostrophe (*their, its, your*). If you add an apostrophe to *its*, as in *it's*, the meaning of the word changes to "it is."

Comma

The comma has five main uses (other than in dates, addresses, and so on):

1. between items in a series

> For the party I bought red, green, yellow, blue, and purple balloons.

2. between independent clauses joined by a coordinating conjunction

> I tried to get pink balloons, but they were sold out.

3. after an introductory clause

> Since the pink balloons were sold out, I decided to return the pink streamers.

4. around anything that gets between the subject and verb

> The salesperson, however, told me the pink balloons would be in on Tuesday.

5. after a conjunctive adverb linking two independent clauses

> The party isn't until Friday; therefore, I'll go back Wednesday for pink balloons.

PROOFREADING

Proofreading sounds easy. Simply read over what you've written and fix the mistakes, right? Unfortunately, it's not that simple, and the reason lies in our brain's great success in coping with what life throws at it, including mistakes in our writing. Find the mistake in this sentence:

> I called up Phil and we made plans to meet at the Tim Hortons at the the corner of Adelaide and Main.

Did you find it? Chances are good that your brain simply ignored the second "the" in that sentence. And that's what makes proofreading difficult. Our brains are really good at compensating for minor errors. In order to proofread effectively, we need to outsmart the brain. Here are two tips:

1. *Try proofreading backward.* I start with the last sentence of my writing and proofread backward, one sentence at a time, moving upward through the page. This seems to short-circuit the brain's tendency to blind me to the errors. Because I'm doing something out of the ordinary, starting at the end and moving to the beginning rather than the usual starting at the top and cruising down, I am able to see what is actually on the page rather than what the brain has filtered for me.
2. *Keep an error log.* Out of the multitude of errors a person could make, each of us seems to have our favourites. While it is important to do a global proofread, looking for all errors, it is helpful to follow that with a proofread that focuses on those favourite mistakes. In order to do that personal proofread, we first need to analyze the patterns of our errors. Go back to pieces of writing you have done throughout your academic career. What types of errors do you seem to have a fondness for? Which types of things have you had to look out for in your rough drafts? What types of corrections have your teachers made?

   Get a small notebook and log the errors. Step back and look at the patterns. Do you usually spell *receive* as *recieve*? Do you tend to put apostrophes in verbs, or overuse commas? Do you confuse *their* and *there*? What are your recurring errors?

Once you've done the analysis, the rest is simple. Each time you write something, do a global proofread, and then check for your personal errors. And each time you get marked writing back, go back to your error log and re-evaluate just what you need to check for.

By paying attention to your personal errors, you may be able to eliminate them for good. If you can't, though—because bad habits are incredibly hard to break—you'll at least be able to ensure that those errors aren't there by the time someone else reads your work.

A NOTE ON GRAMMAR AND SPELL CHECKERS

Word-processing software includes grammar- and spell-check functions. They are useful tools, but use them with caution. Both grammar checkers and spell checkers offer useful suggestions, but they are not foolproof, and they are no substitute for your own judgment. Always, ALWAYS proofread!

APPENDIX B

The following are some of the most commonly confused words in the English language. Review them and always try to avoid making these mistakes in your writing.

accept   *A*ccept means "t*a*ke." It is always a verb.

except   *Ex*cept means "*ex*cluding."

Everyone *except* Mia *accepted* my explanation.

advice   The difference in pronunciation makes the difference in meaning clear.

advise   Ad*vise* (rhymes with *wise*) is a verb. Ad*vice* (rhymes with *nice*) is a noun.

I *advise* you not to listen to free *advice*.

affect   *Affect* as a verb means "influence." As a noun, it means "a strong feeling" (as also seen in a related word, *affection*).

effect   *Effect* is a noun meaning "result." If you can substitute *result*, then *effect* is the word you need. Occasionally, *effect* is used as a verb meaning "to bring about."

Learning about the effects of caffeine affected my coffee-drinking habits.

Depressed people often display inappropriate affect.

Antidepressant medications can *effect* profound changes in mood.

allusion   An *allusion* is an implied or indirect reference.

illusion   An *illusion* is something that appears to be real or true but is not what it seems. It can be a false impression, idea, or belief.

> Many literary *allusions* can be traced to the Bible or to Shakespeare.

> A good movie creates an *illusion* of reality.

are   *Are* is a verb; *our* shows ownership. Confusion of these

our   two words often results from careless pronunciation.

> Where *are our* leaders?

choose   Pronunciation gives the clue here. *Choose* rhymes with *booze* and means "select."

chose   *Chose* rhymes with *rose* and means "selected."

> Please *choose* a topic.

> I *chose* filmmaking.

cite   To *cite* means "to quote from" or "to refer to."

sight   *Sight* is the ability to see, or something that is visible or worth seeing.

site   A *site* is the location of something: a building, a town, or a historic event.

> A lawyer *cites* precedents; writers *cite* their sources in articles or research papers; and my friends *cite* my essays as examples of brilliant writing.

> She lost her *sight* as the result of an accident.

> With his tattoos and piercings, Izzy was a *sight* to behold.

> The *site* of the battle was the Plains of Abraham, which lies west of Quebec City.

coarse   *Coarse* means "rough, unrefined." (Remember: the slang word ***arse*** is co**arse**.)

course   For all other meanings, use *course*.

> That sandpaper is too *coarse* to use on the lacquer finish.

> *Coarse* language only weakens your argument.

> Of *course* you'll do well in a *course* on the history of pop music.

complement   A *complement* completes something.

compliment   A *compliment* is a gift of praise.

> A glass of wine would be the perfect *complement* to the meal.

> Some people are embarrassed by *compliments*.

conscience   Your *conscience* is your sense of right and wrong.

conscious   *Conscious* means "aware" or "awake" (able to feel and think).

> After Ann cheated on the test, her *conscience* bothered her.

> Ann was *conscious* of having done wrong.

> The injured man was *unconscious*.

consul   A *consul* is a government official stationed in another country.

council   A *council* is an assembly or official group. Members of a *council* are *councillors*.

counsel   *Counsel* can be used to mean both "advice" and "to advise."

> The Canadian *consul* in Venice was very helpful.

> The Women's Advisory *Council* meets next month.

> Maria gave me good *counsel*.

> She *counselled* me to hire a lawyer.

desert   A *désert* (with the emphasis on the first *e*) is a dry, barren place. As a verb, *desért* means "leave behind."

dessert   *Dessért* is the part of a meal that you'd probably like a second helping of, so give it a double *s*.

> The tundra is Canada's only *desert* region.

> As soon as our backs were turned, our guard *deserted* his post.

> Ice cream is my children's favourite *dessert*.

forth   *Forth* means "**forward.**"

fourth   *Fourth* contains the number **four,** which gives it its meaning.

> Please stop pacing back and *forth*.

> The Raptors lost their *fourth* game in a row.

hear   *Hear* is what you do with your ears.

here   *Here* is used for all other meanings.

Now *hear* this!

Ranjan isn't *here*.

Here is your assignment.

it's   *It's* is a shortened form of *it is*. The apostrophe takes the place of the *i* in *is*. If you can substitute *it is*, then *it's* is the form you need.

its   If you can't substitute *it is*, then *its* is the correct word. *It's* is also commonly used as the shortened form of *it has*. In this case, the apostrophe takes the place of the *h* and the *a* in *has*.

It's not really difficult. (*It is* not really difficult.)

The book has lost *its* cover. ("The book has lost it is cover" makes no sense, so you need *its*.)

It's been a bad month for software sales.

later   *Later* refers to time and has the word **late** in it.

latter   *Latter* means "the second of two" and has two *t*'s. It is the opposite of *former*.

It is *later* than you think.

You take the former, and I'll take the *latter*.

lead   *Lead* is pronounced to rhyme with *speed* and is the present tense of the verb *to lead*. (*Led* is the past tense of the same verb.)

led   The only time you pronounce *lead* as "led" is when you are referring to the soft, heavy, grey metal used to make bullets or leaded windows.

> You *lead*, and I'll decide whether to follow.

> Your suitcase is so heavy it must be filled with either gold or *lead*.

loose   Pronunciation is the key to these words. *Loose* rhymes with *goose* and means "not tight."

lose   *Lose* rhymes with *ooze* and means "misplace" or "be defeated."

> A *loose* electrical connection is dangerous.

> Some are born to win, some to *lose*.

moral   Again, pronunciation provides the clue you need. *Móral* refers to the understanding of what is right and wrong.

morale   *Moréle* refers to the spirit or mental condition of a person or group.

> Most religions are based on a *moral* code of behaviour.

> Despite his shortcomings, he is basically a *moral* man.

> Low *morale* is the reason for our employees' absenteeism.

personal   *Personal* means "private."

personnel   *Personnel* refers to the group of people working for a particular employer or to the office responsible for maintaining employees' records.

The letter was marked "*Personal* and Confidential."

We are fortunate to have highly qualified *personnel*.

Yasmin works in the *Personnel* Office.

principal   *Principal* means "main."
principle   A *principle* is a rule.

A *principal* is the main administrator of a school.

The federal government is Summerside's *principal* employer.

The *principal* and the interest totalled more than I could pay. (In this case, "the principal" is the main amount of money.)

One of the instructor's *principles* is to refuse to accept late assignments.

quiet   If you pronounce these words carefully, you won't confuse them. *Quiet* has two syllables.

quite   *Quite* has only one.

The chairperson asked us to be *quiet*.

We had not *quite* finished our assignment.

than   *Than* is used in comparisons. Pronounce it to rhyme with *can*.

then   *Then* refers to time and rhymes with *when*.

Karim is a better speller *than* I am.

> He made his decision *then*.

> Tanya withdrew from the competition; *then* she realized the consequences.

their   *Their* indicates ownership.

there   *There* points out something or indicates place. It includes the word here, which also indicates place.

they're   *They're* is a shortened form of *they are*. (The apostrophe replaces the *a* in *are*.)

> It was *their* fault.

> *There* are two weeks left in the term.

> Let's walk over *there*.

> *They're* late, as usual.

too   The *too* with an extra *o* means "more than enough" or "also."

two   *Two* is the number after one.

to   For all other meanings, use *to*.

> She thinks she's been working *too* hard. He thinks so *too*.

> There are *two* sides *to* every argument.

> The *two* women knew *too* much about each other *to* be friends.

were If you pronounce these three carefully, you won't con-fuse them. *Were* rhymes with *fur* and is a verb.

where *Where* is pronounced "wear," includes the word **here,** and indicates place.

we're *We're* is a shortened form of *we are* and is pronounced "weer."

> You *were* joking, *weren't* you?

> *Where* did you want to meet?

> *We're* on our way.

who's *Who's* is a shortened form of *who is* or *who has.* If you can substitute *who is* or *who has* for the *who's* in your sentence, then you have the right spelling.

whose Otherwise, use *whose.*

> *Who's* coming to dinner? (*Who is* coming to dinner?)

> *Who's* been sleeping in my bed? (*Who has* been sleeping in my bed?)

> *Whose* paper is this? ("*Who is* paper" makes no sense, so you need *whose.*)

you're *You're* is a shortened form of *you are.* If you can sub-stitute *you are* for *you're* in your sentence, then *you're* using the correct form.

your If you can't substitute *you are,* use *your.*

> *You're* welcome. (*You are* welcome.)

> Unfortunately, *your* hamburger got burned. ("*You are* hamburger" makes no sense, so *your* is the word you want.)

INDEX

(Entries in *italics* are found in Appendix D)

PROPERTY OF
SENECA COLLEGE
LIBRARIES
YORKGATE CAMPUS